Cover by Michael Matamala (www.matamaladesign.com)

Jondle, Jessica
Roller Skating with Rickets and Other Paradoxes of Life with Genetic Disease / by Jessica Jondle
     ISBN 978-0-578-10027-2

Printed in the United States of America

Roller Skating with Rickets

and Other Paradoxes of Life with Genetic Disease

Jessica Jondle

I am not a doctor, and I am entirely unqualified
to dispense medical advice.

Likewise, this book is not designed to convey the message,
"I did it this way; therefore, you should too."
The rare disease community, just like humanity as a whole,
is made up of individuals with unique needs.

In fact, there is only once piece of advice I will offer:

If you don't believe in miracles, you should.

I believe in miracles.

This book is dedicated to my genetic family, worldwide.
To each of you living with cystinosis: you are a miracle.

Contents

acknowledgements

I always thank my God as I remember you in my prayers.
Philemon 1:4

Thou that hast giv'n so much to me,
give me one thing more, a grateful heart.
George Herbert

Not too many years ago, when I first considered the undertaking of the book that you now hold in your hands, I polled some friends about the best time to write a memoir.

"When you have lived through several world wars," one said.

God willing, that won't happen.

"When you are a disgruntled grandmother tired of knitting sweaters," another said.

I've never been very good at knitting.

"When you start to feel the weight of your own mortality."

Bingo.

And so, in the twenty-ninth year of my existence, I got this grandiose idea that perhaps I could preserve my life—since for the first time, it seemed uncertain how much longer I had—and share with others my perspective on living with hardship if I penned it into a memoir.

As I've traveled on this journey, I've discovered that authoring the rare disease experience is immensely challenging. Although I may have optimistically readied myself for oozing creativity when I first sat down with my pen and paper, the joys and pains of life did not seep out of my pores with nothing more than a little sweat. I had to return to places deep within the confines of my memory and forcibly unearth realities that I had not allowed myself to process.

When I was ready to give up before I ever even began, I opened myself up to the words of yet another wise friend. *In order to write anything that anyone will ever be willing to read,* she said, *you'll have to let your guard down. Reveal heartbreak. Let people in. Confess that though you believe there is a God-given silver lining in everything, sometimes you don't see it until years later. Admit that you find yourself, at times, engulfed in very difficult moments.*

I owe so much to the people who have helped me through these moments and have led me to this conclusion: **Life is full of joy from hardship. Life is full of paradoxes.**

For my mom, who I still remember painstakingly extracting all the liquid from tiny capsules before I could swallow pills: there is no way I would be here without all that you've done for me. You are my most monumental inspiration. You kept me healthy when I was young, you sacrificed time and energy for the numerous appointments and hospitalizations, and you kept your expectations for me high. You took on the unpleasant task of giving me weekly injections when it became necessary, came to the football games I cheered at, and fought the school administration on my behalf—and all at a time when my teenage attitude left much to be desired. You taught me determination and encouraged normalcy. When I became a teacher, I knew I had enormous shoes to fill, and I certainly have yet to fill them. But I know that the reason I keep going back to the classroom, day after day, is that you were the best teacher I ever had.

For my dad, who was my stay-at-home parent until I left for college: because I knew that you would never take cystinosis as an excuse to fail, I was driven to succeed. You devoted yourself to things you probably never envisioned doing for a daughter: you went to the store with each new food phase I went through, you bought milk as if we were stockpiling it for the Apocalypse (even though it would only last a few days), and you picked me up every day after school—and three times a week took me to dialysis for two years, only to have to pick me up again four hours later. It was all that car time—and time spent listening to National Public Radio with you— that encouraged my love for politics and interest in the world around me.

For my sister, who is one of the most beautiful souls I have ever met: you have always been a reflection of Jesus' face in my life. I am grateful to have a very real example of someone who not only talks about her faith, but also lives it out in the every day. I know you put up with a lot when we were growing up. Someday, perhaps on the other side of eternity, I will make it up to you.

For my husband, who first caught my eye when I was ten: I hardly remember a time when you weren't on my mind. Whether it was a teenage crush or the pangs of loneliness during your deployment to the Middle East, you've never strayed far from my thoughts. When you married me, you took on a challenge, for you knew that there would come a point when I would lean on you more heavily than most women do on their husbands. You thought nothing of buttoning my pants when my muscles started failing and my fine motor skills deteriorated, and you transformed *my* life with cystinosis into *our* life with cystinosis. For this and so much more, words fall short of expressing my gratitude.

For the friends who cheered me on when I felt like giving up: you are too numerous to name, but I am grateful for every single one of you. You have given me encouragement, tough love, and the impetus to continue writing.

For the prayer warriors who have always petitioned God on my behalf: I went from resenting it when I was young, to appreciating it as I got older, to most recently and presently, requesting it. I don't believe my circumstances have gotten more dire, but my heart has definitely become more open. When I didn't care to let the Almighty in, you cared enough to ask Him to protect me from harm. I thank you with all my heart.

And finally, for the cystinosis community: you are one of the reasons that I am happy to have the life I do. Could I go back in time and somehow remove the pain caused by cystinosis, I would not do so, for I know that I would be removing the blessings as well. And the blessings, of which you are included, far outweigh the hardship. Through the modern miracle of social networking, I have been connected to people that I have never had the privilege of meeting in person—but even my "virtual" friends have offered me hope and advice, provided me with a forum in which to vent, and given me the opportunity to get to know some of the little ones that I count as my heroes. To you I say: cherish what was given. And fight on.

Jessica Jondle
August 2011

prologue | living with

Flight by machines heavier than air is unpractical and insignificant, if not utterly impossible.

Simon Newcomb

The treatment of the disorder is of little value and the prognosis hopeless.

D.A.J. Williamson

Hospital for Sick Children, London

January 7, 1952

I am afraid of bees. Spiders terrify me, and dark, confined spaces make my heart race. More than anything else, though, I am afraid of dropping out of the sky. I think of this possibility as I turn off my electronic devices and prepare for the departure of my flight from Paris to Istanbul.

I have severe pteromerhanophobia, or a fear of flying. More specifically, I have a fear of falling, but I don't know if there's a phobia term for that. (Could this stem from my eagerness, at the tender age of five, to show off my superhero flying abilities by jumping off a piano bench in front of guests? Perhaps my subsequent broken arm scared the daredevil right out of me. Definitely a question for a therapist.)

I don't know exactly when this fright developed into its current state. Like so many babies and toddlers, I was merely uncomfortable on airplanes when I was very young. Later, when I was in high school and embarked on my first transatlantic flight, I was certainly uneasy at the sight of the display in front of me, the first such screen I had ever encountered that showed my position on the globe. I stared at that airplane, a crude graphic that was tiny and yet still too large for the continents over which it floated, and realized that I was in a place that humans shouldn't be. The monitor would occasionally flash the outside temperature and the plane's altitude, both ridiculous numbers not designed for my survival. As I watched the estimated time of arrival creep closer at a snail's pace, I willed the airplane icon farther, faster, lower, warmer… wishing all the while that our European destination would hurry to greet us. No, it was not fear that overwhelmed me on that flight. It was the feeling that what we were doing was *unnatural*.

My next overseas adventure, this time to Kuwait, was the start of my honest-to-goodness terror in the face of the unfriendly skies. I firmly planted my feet on the cabin floor (which I felt was not very firm at all) and sat, nearly perfectly still, until we reached our destination. On the return flight, this meant eighteen hours in a motionless state: our plane was grounded for several hours for "mechanical repairs" after we were seated, and we had a twelve-hour journey ahead of us. Eighteen hours without moving my legs, using the lavatory, or even simply standing. Clearly, I was spooked.

But it was the trip to New Hampshire for a medical conference that surely sealed my fate as a life-long pteromerhanophobic (for by now I feel certain there is no cure). The first leg of the flight (to our nation's capital) was rough, and it was then that I started my habit of reciting the Lord's Prayer hundreds of times in my head while speeding across continents by myself. Mixed in with my King James Version of the prayer was a bit of, *and if I die before I wake, I pray the Lord my soul to take,* as if the turbulence of the flight was all a bad dream. The bad dream turned to a nightmare when, upon boarding the small plane to head from Washington, D.C. to New Hampshire, the pilot warned us all that it was going to be a bumpy ride. I don't think that flight was very long—perhaps an hour or so—but it was one of the most intense hours of my life. Once we got through the storm, I was never the same.

So it was with much trepidation that I arrived at the airport this morning. It is a trip of a lifetime. Not only am I going to get to meet and speak to the cystinosis community in Turkey, but I am traveling to a part of the world that I have studied and love dearly. The thrill of this adventure somewhat successfully quelled my fear of flying in the month leading up to the trip itself, but the past few nights have been almost entirely devoid of sleep.

As Wayne and I approached the security line, where he would be saying goodbye, I tried to maintain some semblance of optimism. "At least I only have to make it to New York on my own," I told him. "Then I'll be flying with my mom the rest of the way."

And indeed, that had been the plan. I would fly from San Diego to New

York by myself and meet my mom as she arrived on the East Coast from San Francisco. Then, together, we would fly from New York to Istanbul, where we would do a little sightseeing before taking the train to Ankara for the conference. The Cystinosis Foundation asked if I would give a speech, and last night I went over my words one last time:

I am twenty-eight years old and I have cystinosis. We have all heard a plethora of scientific information today, and I know we are all incredibly grateful for the tireless research these doctors have conducted in their respective fields. I would not be where I am today without these efforts. Because of their hard work, I can stand here and give you a perspective of the disease from someone living with it. Maybe for some of you with young children, it will help you as you anticipate what may be to come. There are many unknowns with this disease, but I stand here knowing this: I have been blessed.

When I was growing up, my family attended cystinosis conferences, much like this one, on a regular basis. This became a time when I could see people like me. Sometimes, this was a challenge. Sometimes I didn't want to be reminded that I was sick. But a lot of times it was also a relief to be myself, and know that everyone would understand. It wouldn't be necessary to explain to anyone why I took pills, or why I drank so much water and couldn't stand the heat. I could play with people my age without those social barriers that could sometimes separate me from the kids at my school. For these reasons, I am excited for this very first Cystinosis Conference of the Eastern Mediterranean. For some of you, this may be your first time seeing someone else with cystinosis. Though we are all different—not only in our CTNS gene mutations but also in our daily lives—with a disease this rare, the simple fact that we share cystinosis makes us family.

I studied Middle Eastern culture, religion, language, and politics at the University of California, Berkeley. Something I came to appreciate about the culture over the course of my studies is the strong sense of family and community. It is exciting to see that a new family is being formed here in Ankara—and although hundreds of miles may separate your hometowns, you will always be connected to the people in this room after this conference ends. For those of us with cystinosis, it is the joy of having a new family member who knows what life with the disease is like. For parents, it is the security of having another parent to call when your child is sick and you need a listening ear or advice on what may come next. For doctors, it is an opportunity to come together and share potentially life-saving research. In Arabic, there is a phrase that I love—and that I feel has no strong English counterpart: Inshah'allah, *often translated "God willing." I have always found comfort in that phrase (except, perhaps, when my Arabic professor would say, "There will be a test on Monday,* inshah'allah*"). But in all seriousness, I hope there will be a lot of* inshah'allah*s at this conference.* Inshah'allah, *friends will be made.* Inshah'allah, *we will learn something from each other.* Inshah'allah, *steps will be taken toward finding a cure for cystinosis.* Inshah'allah *reflects my deeply held belief that it was God's will to touch each person in this room with a rare, special condition.*

In the Bible, there is a verse that states that "every good and perfect gift is from above." While perfect bodies do not exist in this world, I do believe that the blessings of cystinosis have been perfect gifts from God. That is right—to me, cystinosis is a blessing. It doesn't define us, but it does refine us. Cystinosis has taught me how much fun it is to overcome challenges. Cystinosis has taught me empathy for the sick and disadvantaged. You may have read in the news about the turmoil over health care raging in America. While I think there are no easy answers, I believe my own battles have taught me that people with preexisting conditions face challenges that can be both disheartening and hazardous to their health. Cystinosis has taught me to think twice before I judge. Cystinosis has taught me that depression is very real. It has taught me that life is full of obstacles. It has taught me that obstacles are designed to be surmounted. Cystinosis has given me the opportunity to be awed by modern medicine. Even more so, cystinosis has increased my faith and given me the opportunity to be awed by the power of prayer.

What I hope you all walk away from this conference with is the knowledge that cystinosis is a manageable disease, and not one that seals some sort of awful fate. Most days, I don't give it a second thought. I had a transplant ten years ago, went to the University of California, Berkeley and studied the Middle East and Arabic, worked full-time as an editor, a writer, and most recently, a teacher. I married my high school sweetheart two years ago and am working on my master's degree in education. I love middle school students, history, writing, foreign films, a good political debate, and Jesus. And I happen to have cystinosis. Sometimes I forget that. I take pills and I put eye drops in my eyes. But all of these things are second nature, and don't get much thought throughout the day. I don't anticipate a time when cystinosis will hold me back.

So I stand before you today, with my head held high, not because I am proud of what I have done—but because I am proud of how I was created. With a genetic defeat perhaps intended for evil, but used for good. Inshah'allah, cystinosis will be a blessing for you, too.

As I reexamine this speech on my flight to Istanbul, I reflect on how life rarely turns out the way we think it will. I have lived with cystinosis for my entire existence, but I never knew that it would become such an important part of who I am and lead me to share my appreciation for it with others. Likewise, I didn't expect to find myself traveling from San Diego, California, USA to Istanbul, Turkey (via Paris, France) alone due to unforeseen delays. I silently curse the wind as we hit a patch of turbulence.

In contrast to my mere discomfort when I was young, now I fear falling out of the sky on an almost daily basis. Even when there is very little likelihood that I will be getting on an airplane in the near future, I am susceptible to graphic nightmares that leave me shaken and paranoid. On those rare occasions that I do fly, such as now, I have come to depend on downing a strong drink about a half hour prior to takeoff, as physician-prescribed remedies have been ineffective in staving off panic attacks. Woe is he who travels with me (typically my husband) and lends me his hand to hold; in my most anxious moments, my nails can draw blood. I live in fear that I will meet my end falling out of an airplane, from heights of unnatural proportions.

The irony hits me as the pilot comes on the intercom to alert us to our descent into Istanbul. It is very unlikely that I will die falling out of the sky. My phobia prevents me from even boarding a plane unless it is absolutely necessary; if I can get to my destination by car, train, bus, boat, camel, teleportation, or other method, then that's the way I'll go. And in my rational mind, I know that airplanes are safer than many of these other modes of transportation, even though in my more emotional heart I don't believe in aerodynamics.

No, the irony is that I have a fatal disease, that—barring some tragic accident (a plane crash, perhaps?)—will kill me. I may rarely embark on air travel, but my body daily fights a losing battle.

Even so, I think as I disembark and prepare to navigate the sea of people to obtain a visa and find my mom, *this is a story of victory.*

ruminations from the rink

I started this prologue with quoted perspectives on two different impossibilities: that of human flight and that of treating cystinosis. Clearly, I have too much in common with Mr. Newcomb, though it took a while for my fear to fully develop. On the other hand, I have lived my entire life in steady, consistent, and unknowing opposition to Dr. Williamson.

When writing about cystinosis in 1952, Williamson reported that the seven-and-a-half-year-old patient who served as the subject of his paper was *dying of* her condition. I suppose this is true; however, aren't we all dying of our own condition, our own existence? Whether healthy or ill, each day brings us closer to our deaths; with the passing years our bodies fight against us—and we are losing.

But in any situation, I prefer to see myself as *living with* my condition. The paradox, then, is that **we are all living with what we are dying from.** A small rhetoric shift changes all of our stories to stories of victory.

What are you dying from that you should be living with? Out of my fear of flying came a life-changing trip to Turkey. Out of my cystinosis comes joy in light of God's grace. What blessings have you been given through hardship?

Rolling forward…

one | harmonious hearts, hostile dna

This founder mutation... apparently occurred in Germany in approximately A.D. 500 and spread by migration to neighboring regions.

Drs. Gahl, Thoene, and Schneider
New England Journal of Medicine, 2002

Love is a kind of warfare.

Ovid

Happily ever afters. These are the ends that justify the multifarious means of countless stories laden with fantasy.

Reality, though, is always more interesting. I can't claim that this is genuine, but this is how my firmly grounded imagination likes to fabricate it.

✧   ✧   ✧   ✧   ✧

It is a tumultuous time in Europe. The city of Rome, invaded multiple times in the past century, has at last endured her final assault. The city is in ruins, and throughout the former Roman Empire, change is afoot. The so-called *barbarians*—people given the unflattering label by the Romans, who for years looked down upon the Germanic tribes pushing on her Empire's borders as uncouth and uncivilized—are slowly forming a new political order in Europe. Each town, village, and port city has its own unique recent chronology of insecurity and warfare.

The countryside near the town of Trier, once known as Augusta Treverorum and located at the outer reaches of the former Empire, is not an exception. As the Germanic tribes made it their mission in previous decades to ravage Roman lands, the countryside had presented itself as the easiest target. Imperial troops had remained in Augusta Treverorum itself for as long as possible before finally succumbing, not to the military superiority of the Germanic peoples, but to their numbers and brute force.

But even in times of instability, survival requires food. Ebregisel is unaware of his rightful king, but he knows that the land won't farm itself. (Feudalism has not yet taken shape in the Germanic kingdoms, but a type of proto-feudalism is quickly becoming the norm.) His grandfather had lived during a time when the pursuit of war was considered both manly and glorious, but now Ebregisel's life is dominated by planting, harvesting, and sending up prayers to the Christian God that the weather will cooperate so that he can pay his dues to the local authorities and still have enough left over to help feed his ailing parents.

In a village near Ebregisel's farmstead, Beretrude lives with her family. Their austere existence sees them spending a considerable amount of time bartering for their necessities, as coins have long since gone out of circulation. Beretrude's father is a potter, forming simple kitchenware items for the townspeople with his bare hands. The young Beretrude, only nearly out of her teens, has heard stories of a time not so long ago when wheel-spun pottery and exquisite tableware were produced in La Graufesenque in southern Gaul and distributed hundreds of miles away and throughout the provincial lands managed by Rome, including Trier and the surrounding area. She has even heard it said that this pottery used to be found in the most humble homes of peasants, where tiled ceilings looked down upon the dining table! Beretrude has never seen a Roman tile or piece of pottery, but she is certain that they must have been wonderful.

But the post-Roman state that Beretrude and Ebregisel now live in is a direct result of their not-so-distant ancestors, the migrating Germanic Franks and Burgundians, entering the land and making it their own. In a lot of ways, daily life for the peasantry is relatively unchanged. The ever-present possibility of disquietude, though, makes emigration to other lands a persistent prospect.

Through a chance meeting when Ebregisel goes to the village in search of materials for a new yolk for his plough, the two young people encounter one another and begin their journey into love. He is drawn to Beretrude's fair skin; she adores his unusual blue eyes. At some point in their less-than-picturesque lives, he asks for her hand in marriage. That he is able to choose his bride is a privilege unique to their low peasant status; with no wealth comes no need for the parental negotiations so typical of upper-class marriages of the time.

Of course she says yes. How could she not? Though they are both poor, at that moment, they feel like royalty. They are each marrying perfection, and all that can possibly result is pure bliss.

Deoxyribonucleic acid, or DNA, is a term and a concept completely foreign to this pair. They have no idea that *genes* and *perfection* have no place in the same sentence, and that they are each similar in ways that will bring about trouble for generations to come. No, as they bask in the beauty of young love, Ebregisel and Beretrude have no idea that it would have been better if they had never met.

Or would it have been? Is it possible to find fulfillment in spite of intense hardship? To step out of the story for a moment, I must opine that everything I've lived and experienced has told me... yes.

As is customary in sixth century Europe, Beretrude is expected to have children. After all, what else is there for a woman to do besides perpetuate her husband's name?

And so they begin their family. With each healthy infant's birth, they thank God for His blessings and providence. There are a couple of babies with normal deliveries who later die at an early age, but this is far from uncommon for the time. Ebregisel and Beretrude mourn, but think nothing serious of it; after all, there are women who lose nearly every child they conceive.

One child in particular, though, wins over his mother's heart. Smaller and more frail than his surviving brothers, he behaves in much the same way as two of the children who died before the age of five. Like his less fortunate siblings, he is late to crawl and late to walk. He eats little but is excessively thirsty. He squints and complains of pain in the sunlight and has difficulty merely walking when his peers are running, playing games, and helping their fathers with farm work. This little one becomes a point of contention between his mother and father, for Ebregisel finds him to be next to useless and scolds him for his laziness.

Beretrude, however, suspects that it is not laziness that keeps the child from pulling his weight on the farm. She correctly assumes that all of these symptoms—the slowness to walk, the thirst, the sensitivity to light, the emaciated appearance and short stature, the bowing in his legs—are connected. She even suspects that these symptoms are part of a larger illness that killed two of her previous children; *but this one, by the grace of God,* she reminds herself, *has survived.*

His mother's fondness grows. What perhaps makes the human species unique is that rather than reject the runt of our litter, we often endow him with additional love, time, and affection. It is our instinct to nurse him to health rather than leave him to fend for himself and inevitably meet defeat. Unwilling that anyone fail under our watchful gaze, we combat his lemony lot with attempts to make only the sweetest of lemonade for him to enjoy.

Such is the story of the one who survives. When he is too tired or in too much agony to walk, even at the age of nine, his mother carries him. When he refuses to eat, she sets aside extra milk for him, for the boy always seems parched. When he complains of pain in his eyes, his mother uses the folds of her peasant skirt to shield him from the sun.

She alone sees his potential, his cleverness, his strength. While people in the village speak of him as worthless or as evidence of God's dissatisfaction with his parents, she knows he is stronger than any of the boys pushing heavy ploughs to till the soil of family farms. It is a rare occasion indeed that this mother and son are not together.

In sixth century Europe, if your offspring live past early childhood, there is a certain degree of assurance that they will be around for years to come. But Ebregisel and Beretrude see their son getting worse and worse. When they bury him at the age of ten, his mother is heartbroken.

This couple is fortunate. In spite of the difficult circumstances of the time, they live into old age and are around to see their remaining children grow up and find love and have families of their own. Life remains hard, and the mother never forgets her son who died upon completion of his first decade of life. When her daughter loses a child with similar symptoms at six years of age, the elder matriarch finds herself wondering again if there is something unique about her family.

But she keeps her thoughts to herself, for at the time, it is not a woman's place to speak out about physical ailments and their causes—causes that only the Almighty can know. And so her knowledge dies with her, forgotten by those who knew it, never uncovered by those who didn't.

Generation after generation come and go. Some descendants of Ebregisel and Beretrude lose children to similar symptoms, but most have perfectly healthy offspring. They migrate throughout northern Europe, and many move to Brittany, France, finding a slightly better life than that in the Rhineland. The mysterious illness that takes children in some families but not others is never discussed, for its rarity and a relative lack of medical knowledge lead people to merely accept their fate rather than fight it.

It is on this backdrop that I tell the story of a more modern couple, two Americans who have forgotten their heritage. The man knows that his last name, Britt, is a nod to where his ancestors had lived before him—Brittany, France. But like many people in the 1970s, he knows not what effect his heritage might have on his DNA.

The couple's first child is a perfect blessing in every way. Blond, fair-skinned, and blue-eyed, she captures their hearts immediately. A clever and social child, she intensely studies the world around her.

It soon becomes evident that this child would do well to have a sibling, for someone with so much love to give to others should not be left alone. And so, her parents eventually find themselves eagerly awaiting the birth of child number two.

Like her sister, this child is born with fair skin and beautiful blond hair. When she arrives on July 14, 1981, she is a healthy, nine-pound baby. It isn't long, though, before it becomes clear that this child is different. She stops growing. She ignores food. She needs a seemingly constant supply of water and begs to be carried long after she should be walking. She rubs her eyes often and is bothered by the sun.

This second daughter is also a perfect blessing. It just takes a special love to see it that way. And for the girl herself, it takes decades to understand and accept her position as a beautiful child of God.

I am this ever-blessed, but only newly understanding child.

ruminations from the rink

The paradox is not that the old adage that *opposites attract* is really true—but that sometimes we are attracted to those who share genetic similarities that can wreak havoc with our offspring. **From loving harmony comes toxic life—life that is inherently flawed and yet immeasurably beautiful.**

In truth, very little is known about the origins of cystinosis. One of the common mutations of the CTNS gene—the 57-kb deletion—has been traced to Germany around the year 500, during a time when people were spreading out throughout the former Roman Empire. It wasn't until 1903, however, that the symptoms were collected and labeled as Abderhalden-Kaufmann-Lignac syndrome after the three most influential scientific professionals who studied them. Initially mistakenly categorized as cystinuria—a disorder in which the amino acid cystine accumulates in the urine and crystallizes into stones—over the course of the first few decades of the twentieth century, Abderhalden-Kaufmann-Lignac syndrome was recognized as a unique disease, cystinosis.

Cystinosis is a defect in the lysosomes, or parts of the cell that hold enzymes that break down cellular waste such as proteins and acids. In particular, the lysosomal transporter *cystinosin* fails to eliminate the amino acid cystine from the cells, which leads to a dangerous accumulation of cystine and subsequent cell damage. This in turn creates problems in multiple systems, with the kidneys often being the first to fail. Cystine buildup in the eyes can cause photophobia (light sensitivity), painful sensations (almost as if there is dust in the eyes), and blindness. Children and adolescents with cystinosis may also have continuing bone problems and a general lack of energy.

Later in life, adults with cystinosis may experience extensive muscle wasting, difficulty swallowing, thyroid disease, and complications in all organs of the body, including the brain. There is no cure for cystinosis, and it is considered terminal.

As an autosomal recessive disease, cystinosis can only be passed on when both parents are carriers. When this is the case, both mother and father have one affected gene and one unaffected gene. This results in a twenty-five percent chance of any offspring of the couple having the disease: a child can either inherit one healthy gene from each parent and thus be neither a person with the disease nor a carrier (one in four chance); he can inherit a healthy gene from either parent and an affected gene from the other, resulting in carriership (two in four); or the child can inherit both faulty genes, resulting in the acquisition of the disease itself (one in four).

Because the likelihood of two carriers having a child together is so slim, cystinosis is incredibly rare. While cystinosis affects approximately 1 in 100,000-200,000 births in areas where the genetic condition is known to exist, the occurrence is higher (about 1 in 26,000) in Brittany, France.

Our genes are littered with mistakes and defects, and cystinosis is only one of a multitude of potential resultant diseases. While cystinosis carrier testing is possible prior to making the decision to have children, it is impractical (and expensive) to get checked for every disease-carrying gene that we might pass on. Inevitably, from the emotional and physical love that exists between two people will come genetic hostility.

I have heard it said repeatedly over the course of my life that having a child with cystinosis is a tragedy. There are those who hate the disease and feel guilty for bringing additional suffering into the world, especially the world of a child. This is a perplexing point of view for me, especially given the subjective and personal nature of the word *suffering*.

Maybe our genes are at war, but my world is one that is filled with healing blessings that wouldn't exist without cystinosis. Like the fictitious child of Ebregisel and Beretrude, I am a unique creation and the object of abounding love.

I wouldn't change a thing.

Rolling forward...

two | roller skating with rickets

No victor believes in chance.

Friedrich Nietzsche

At close to a year of age, I stop growing.

This is at first dismissed as a simple act of nature finding its equilibrium. My size at birth put me in the ninety-ninth percentile; now, surely, it is time for me to ease my way into a more desirable range on the growth chart.

But troubling behaviors are beginning to emerge. I stop eating. I walk at seventeen months, but then seem to revert back to my earlier preference for being carried everywhere. I begin to develop a hollow, sickly look in my eyes.

It is April 19, 1983—three months before my second birthday. My mom and I arrive at Letterman Army Medical Center just before noon, and I am promptly admitted to Room 514W. Several doctors stop by, but Dr. Kerry takes the lead in organizing my care and determining the cause of my failure to thrive. He says the tests given today are to see if maybe my whole problem is a chronic urinary tract infection. Wouldn't that be a relief!

The nurses marvel at the adorable (if I do say so myself) twenty-one-month-old little girl and tell my mother that they hope we will be headed home soon.

My hands, legs, and abdomen are x-rayed for bone age. Blood and urine are collected. I am grumpy, sick, and exhausted, and by late afternoon I will have nothing of the catheter and bag the nurses want to position for a twenty-four-hour urine collection.

My lack of cooperation eventually results in my little body being tied to the bed. I protest with my voice and my free hands, but I come to understand that resistance truly is futile. I don't fall asleep until several hours later, with my mother sleeping on the floor beside me; despite the potential seriousness of my condition, the hospital is unable to produce a cot for her to sleep on. I am too young to understand that she would slumber standing up if it were required of her—I just know that I don't want her to leave my side.

I remain strapped to the bed throughout the night and for much of the next day, only released briefly to have an eye examination in the ophthalmology department.

"I'm looking for cystinosis," Dr. Frey tells my mother as I sit in the oversized evaluation chair. "It's a biochemical disease that exists when there is too much cystine in the system due to non-functioning kidneys." She makes a note of the disease's name in her new spiral-bound medical log, planning to look it up at the library later.

(In fact, my parents will subsequently find that Dr. Frey's definition isn't entirely accurate, but as the disease garners at best a couple sentences in only the most comprehensive of ophthalmology textbooks, it is hardly surprising.)

Dr. Frey adds that he has been told that I have renal tubular acidosis. My mom is thankful to have a piece of conclusive information, even if she is unclear of its meaning. Apparently, cystinosis is sometimes an underlying cause of renal tubular acidosis and he wants to rule it out.

I flinch at the discomfort of having a bright light shined in my eyes. Fortunately, his examination ends shortly after it begins.

"Her eyes are clear," he says, somewhat triumphantly. "She does not have cystinosis or any other eye-related condition. Her physicians will have to investigate other causes."

In fact, by the next day—April 21—Dr. Kerry announces that many additional tests are needed. As I surrender more of my blood for a chromosome study and just barely tolerate another catheter placement for a urine collection, I am unaware that I am experiencing more medical turmoil before the age of two than most people endure in a decade.

Ammonium chloride is pumped into my tiny body—it upsets me greatly and I fight the nurses and doctors who struggle to administer it. According to Dr. Kerry, this acid-loading test will measure my kidneys' effectiveness in maintaining a proper acid-base balance; my blood and urine will be sampled later to see how acidic they are. A reasonable enough test, my tenacity in the face of the health professionals' efforts nonetheless results in the punishment I have come to almost expect: I am once again strapped to the hospital gurney. But despite not being the exact epitome of comfort, the bed offers me the familiarity that I so desperately need after a full morning of poking and prodding. I fall asleep immediately, completely oblivious to the lunch that remains untouched beside me.

Undisturbed dreams, though, are a luxury on a busy hospital floor, especially when you are the mysterious subject of many would-be detectives in doctors' clothing. Dr. Chester, a kidney expert, comes to see me in the early afternoon.

"She'll be fine," he tells my mother in the reassuring voice that interrupted my slumber. "If it is what I think it is, treatment will take care of the problem right away."

I don't know if my mom is skeptical at this prediction, but I am certainly restless. I want my own bed. My favorite blanket. The family Burmese cat, Neko. If I could understand, I would feel hopeful at Dr. Chester's words simply because I want them to be true.

He describes what he believes to be the issue. "The kidneys are not taking the acid out of her system and she has too much of it in her body, so it is being absorbed wherever it can. The bones happen to be getting the bulk of the acid and are being softened as a result. We call this *rickets,* which are often due to a vitamin D deficiency but in Jessica's case are more likely caused by a general imbalance."

"So she is more acidic than a normal child?" My mom understands what he is saying, but is craving an answer to the obvious question—what caused this?

"Essentially, yes. Our bodies are made up of acid and alkaline. It's an important balance that is maintained in a normal person. Jessica has too much acid, and so she must take a solution of bicarbonate on a daily basis, perhaps for the rest of her life. This solution will balance her system and repair her bones."

He leaves without answering—*why is this happening?*

Several hours later, Dr. Kerry sees us in the hallway and comes over to announce that he thinks a diagnosis can be made with the data available. Although the blood drawn for the chromosome study won't be analyzed until tomorrow due to limitations in the lab, he knows what to look for: Turner Syndrome or Turner Mosaic.

My parents don't find this news very encouraging, and as they do a little research, they find that usually children with Turner Syndrome have distinctive features, with a webbed neck and short stature being the most prominent. But in Turner Mosaic, the only physical abnormality is short stature. At the very least, Dr. Kerry believes it is worth ruling these conditions out.

When the new urine test comes back, though, a dramatic change is noted with the earlier addition of the ammonium chloride. The results seem to indicate that the renal proximal tubules are not reabsorbing bicarbonate to counter, or buffer, the acid. Dr. Kerry says I therefore most certainly have renal tubular acidosis, which is also keeping calcium, phosphorus, and potassium from my bones and making my legs unnaturally short. The new plan is to give me additional bicarbonate and potassium orally in order to make up for what my body simply refuses to hold on to. The dosage will be monitored until my levels look healthy.

"With normalized amounts of bicarbonate and potassium in Jessica's system, her condition should correct itself," Dr. Kerry explains.

My mom eagerly shares this information with the regular family pediatrician when he stops by. Like Dr. Kerry, he notes that careful monitoring will be required to find out how much supplementation I really need.

The next morning, much to my chagrin, I am once again bagged for urine collection and more blood is drawn. *When will this end?*

Multiple doctors drop in to visit the cute toddler in Room 514W, all offering their thoughts. Dr. Bradley, a physician who treated my ear infection three weeks ago, wonders aloud about the underlying condition.

Other doctors feel certain I will need vitamin D and phosphates in addition to bicarbonate and potassium. My renal tubular acidosis is depleting my system of some of the basic elements needed for survival. I am literally peeing out, rather than reabsorbing, essential nutrients. Another practitioner notes that one of the tests revealed protein is also spilling into my urine.

Throughout all this, my family, particularly my mom, is desperate for answers. Whereas I just want the pokes and prods to cease and to return to my own comfortable bed, she doesn't want to leave the hospital without a satisfying, conclusive diagnosis. I have renal tubular acidosis and probably something called Fanconi syndrome; both of these conditions are having a dangerous effect on my bones. But these syndromes are typically part of some larger diagnosis and do not spontaneously occur in a healthy child. By that afternoon, Dr. Kerry sits down with us and offers a more thorough explanation of what is going on.

"There are two forms of renal tubular acidosis," he says, "proximal and distal. Because the ammonium chloride test revealed that Jessica isn't absorbing bicarbonate, we can conclude that she has the proximal form. That is why treating her with bicarbonate will help."

My mom ponders this. Prior to my hospitalization, her experience with bicarbonate was limited to Alka-Seltzer, which she knows is an antacid used to treat heartburn. "What does bicarbonate do?"

"It serves as a buffer to keep the amount of acid in our bodies in check. Jessica is in a chronic state of acidosis, so she's not growing. There may be other reasons as well, but that is the main one. She doesn't have a urinary tract infection, but her kidneys are not working too well. We believe she has Fanconi syndrome, but the condition is not distinctly genetic or chromosomal—it is merely the name used for a specific proximal problem."

"So the Fanconi causes her to lose bicarbonate through her urine?"

"Yes, and it can also result in a loss of other things—sugar, protein, amino acids, phosphates—and we suspect this might be the case with Jessica. We'll know more conclusively when the twenty-four-hour urine test comes back. We do need to find the underlying cause. Since her eyes are normal, we've ruled out cystinosis, which can be a cause of Fanconi syndrome."

My mom sighs deeply. She is so appreciative of Dr. Kerry's hard work and determination in finding out what is wrong with me, but she is getting weary. "When do you think we'll know the underlying cause and will be able to go home?" she asks.

For his part, Dr. Kerry sees the toll all of this is taking on our family. "We can do more tests on an outpatient basis, and as the results come back more medication will be given to her. We do want to find out if the condition existed from birth. Right now her parathyroid is working overtime to do the job that the kidneys aren't doing, and as the medication is given and her kidneys kick in again, the parathyroid may decide to stop working and so she'll have to be monitored closely. X-rays show that her bone age is about fifteen months, and we want to see improvement there as well."

He notices the lines of worry on my mother's face. "All through this she should be fine, Gayle. We might be able to give her something called Shohl's solution to improve her body chemistry and make her feel a lot better. I don't know how long she'll need to supplement with bicarbonate—maybe a year, maybe ten years, maybe forever—but she *will* get better with treatment."

"And in the mean time, you will continue looking for the primary condition?"

"Yes. Fanconi syndrome is not hereditary but might be caused by something hereditary. We will find it. I am compiling all my notes on Jessica's case and will be putting them in her medical record. You should have a copy of everything—if you are out of town and have reason to see a doctor, you will need to produce Jessica's records because her case is complicated."

My mom is exhausted. She thanks Dr. Kerry and turns to leave his office.

"Oh, and Gayle," Dr. Kerry calls to her, "the bicarbonate might make Jessica burp and fart a lot."

She briefly allows herself a smile as she heads back to Room 514W.

My pediatrician comes by with a recipe for my medicine. My parents sample it. It tastes so awful that they just know it will be a challenge to get me to take it. We are discharged from the hospital and headed home to await further instructions. Dr. Kerry calls two hours later and tells my mom to return the next day for yet another blood sample. He has spoken with someone at the University of California, San Francisco (UCSF) Medical Center and believes he might know what the underlying cause is. He doesn't want to say more until he makes sure with a few more tests.

On April 23, 1983, my mom and I arrive at Letterman at 10:00 a.m. so that I can give more blood. I'm getting good at this—I merely watch the needle with boredom as it enters my arm.

Later that day, I am given my first dose of Shohl's, a solution designed to correct my electrolyte imbalance. My parents use the following recipe:

35 cc Shohl's
35 cc frozen sweetened grape juice concentrate
70 cc water
1 teaspoon sugar

I drink it easily. It's delicious! I get a potassium solution about an hour later. It is not nearly as palatable and I balk at the taste.

For the next few days, we fall into a routine. I drink the Shohl's solution three times a day, at 7:30 a.m., 12:30 p.m., and 6:00 p.m. I take the potassium once a day, but am less than enthusiastic about it and often spill it.

Dr. Kerry calls and asks for urine samples from everyone in the family: my mom, my dad, and my older sister, Kirsten. He wants to see if my condition is familial.

When my mom drops the specimens off at the hospital on April 26, she and I also meet with Dr. Chester, Dr. Kerry, my regular pediatrician, and two other physicians. Each doctor samples my medicine concoction with interest.

"We may need to add vitamin D and calcium to her mixture," Dr. Kerry notes. "We'll try to have the pharmacy make a special *Jessica Britt solution.* Hopefully the pharmacist can remove the sodium from the bicarbonate and the chloride from the potassium and then add vitamin D and calcium. We'll need to continue testing her levels as we try to find the correct balance."

This all sounds very complicated to my mom. "How long will she need to take this?" She is worried that she already knows the answer.

Sure enough, the doctors agree that my condition is probably lifelong. They haven't yet determined if it is congenital or not, as Fanconi syndrome can be either—again, it all depends on the cause. They are still awaiting results of many of the tests from my time in the hospital.

The medicine is bloating me, and my pediatrician discusses the possibility of adding a diuretic to my regimen. However, he points out that diuretics tend to have a potassium-wasting effect on the body—the last thing I need right now! He draws some blood to test my potassium and electrolytes. My potassium comes back in the normal range, but my electrolytes are dangerously low. He and Dr. Kerry both put pressure on the pharmacy to created a more concentrated solution—and fast.

Life continues. I feel somewhat better, though I still demand to be carried everywhere. The rickets in my legs make walking too painful.

April showers give way to May flowers (though in the Bay Area the rain often lingers for a while longer), and we are still unaware of what is causing my myriad health problems. Now just two months shy of my second birthday, I enjoy playing with my sister, long naps, and, despite my bone troubles, roller skating. I have to wonder if I enjoy the sport so much because it is something we do as a family outside of the home—and away from my medicine.

The rickets still haven't improved, and my height has actually decreased slightly. It is evident that I am not reabsorbing phosphates. My bones need help. X-rays reveal irregular borders and a washed-out appearance. Dense, heavy lines show erosion; my bones almost look as though they have been chewed up. The tips of my fingers on my left hand are barely visible on the x-ray and my ribs present a lovely rosary pattern and even feel like a string of beads to the touch. The body has a wonderful way of regulating itself, although in my case, this is coming at a price—in an effort to normalize the calcium level in my blood, my parathyroid is sending a signal to draw the much-needed nutrient from my bones.

Dr. Kerry decides that in addition to overloading my kidneys with calcium in hopes that some of it will go to the bones, he would like me to see the ophthalmologist again. Things just aren't adding up and he wants to revisit the possibility that I have cystinosis.

My parents are not thrilled by this news, but desperate for a diagnosis. My dad investigates cystinosis in the large medical volumes of our local library's reference section. There isn't much, but what he finds isn't good. With symptomatic treatment of Fanconi syndrome, children with cystinosis can live ten years. It is very serious. Renal transplant will eventually be necessary but it is unknown how much this will extend the life of the individual. It is hard to look at the word *cystinosis* and not see the phrase *death sentence.*

There is one troubling detail about positively identifying the disease that catches my parents' attention: in order to make an ophthalmological diagnosis, the eyes have to be examined via slit lamp as the cystine crystals are not typically visible by the naked eye.

Armed with this new information, my mom and I return to ophthalmology. This time, the doctor looks at my eyes with a microscope and slit lamp due to my mom's insistence.

And this time, tiny cystine crystals are found.

The eye doctor assures my mom that the crystals will not impair my vision. My mom asks if there is a medication that might remove the cystine from my eyes. He tells her that regrettably, there is no treatment.

Several doctors from the ophthalmology department look at my eyes before deciding to have a meeting behind closed doors. When they emerge, they tell us that I will need to be sedated so that my eyes can be examined more thoroughly. My parents question the necessity of this, but decide it is something that can be brought up with Dr. Kerry before my new ophthalmology appointment, set for May 12.

When Dr. Kerry hears the news, he explains that my age can hinder the ability to get a good, clear image without sedation. He also tells us that now that cystine has been found, we will need to regroup. My case will be presented at UCSF Medical Center and he will investigate what treatments are available. In the interim, he tells us to drop the Shohl's solution and switch to a liquid medicine called polycitra, which has less sodium and supposedly tastes better (I beg to differ). The drug contains twice as much potassium as I am on currently, so it will serve as my all-in-one medication for now. I'll take 50 cc a day spread into three doses—20, 20, and 10 (this will be raised several times in the coming weeks). The only additional drug he prescribes is a small vitamin D capsule—Rocaltrol—that my mom will need to open and sprinkle in food or juice. Calcium and phosphates are still being considered.

The plan is to go to the pediatric department on the day of my eye appointment and receive chloral hydrate, a sedative. I'll be wheeled to ophthalmology, where the doctor will put drops in my eyes and wait for me to go to sleep. Dr. Kerry will be present at the examination.

A week before the eye exam, I see Dr. Kerry as an outpatient for a routine checkup and update—although by now, nothing related to my health is routine.

"We are going to treat Fanconi syndrome at this time," Dr. Kerry explains, "and not cystinosis. The treatments for cystinosis are not effective, and although lab results may show short-term improvement, the end result is the same. Cystine can go everywhere—the pancreas, the thyroid, and of course, the kidneys. Jessica's hasn't gone too far yet. There is no problem in the glomerulus as of right now; her condition is in the tubule part of the nephron."

My parents are distraught. "Is it in both kidneys? What is the 'end result' of her condition?"

"The problem is bilateral—in both kidneys. The outcomes of cystinosis are renal transplant or death from renal failure. When Jessica starts to show trouble in the glomerulus via a problematic glomerular filtration rate, we will know that her condition has taken a turn for the worse and the time for transplant is coming. There will be time to find a donor."

This is all so much to take in. "How does this happen?" My mom is wondering if there is anything she could have done.

Dr. Kerry phrases his response carefully. "If she indeed has cystinosis, it comes from an autosomal recessive gene. That means that both of you, as her parents, are carriers. In theory, if you were to have four children, one would have cystinosis, one would not have cystinosis or be a carrier, and two would be carriers. It is genetic in much the same way that blond hair and blue eyes are genetic, and in fact, these characteristics often go along with having cystinosis."

"But her eyes are brown. Her sister has blond hair and blue eyes."

"I would like Kirsten's eyes to be checked for crystals as well."

"Is there any chance that Jessica does not have cystinosis?"

"In some rare instances, the cystine is present in the eyes but not in the body. It is still cystinosis in those cases, but it is purely ocular and relatively benign. We will have to do more tests for a definitive diagnosis. I'll find out more when I present her case to some knowledgeable people at UCSF Medical Center." Dr. Kerry is pulling for me. He will do everything he can to make sure I get the best care possible. He even gives my parents his home phone number.

My mom carries me out of the hospital that day with a lot of new information to digest. Cystinosis. Genetic. Even if she had opted for an amniocentesis while pregnant, the result would have been the same. Nothing could have prevented this.

My sedation and subsequent eye exam a few days later are uneventful. It serves only to reinforce what was previously discovered: I have cystine crystals spread around my eyes. Kirsten's eyes, thankfully, are clear.

Dr. Kerry has new information for us. He has found a cystinosis expert, Dr. Jerry Schneider, located at the University of California, San Diego (UCSD). Dr. Schneider is currently experimenting with treatments for cystinosis—treatments beyond the standard supplementation of phosphates, potassium, and electrolytes. Dr. Kerry is fairly certain that I have classic, or infantile nephropathic cystinosis (and not merely an ocular manifestation of the disease), but he wants to make absolutely certain before going forward with any experimental medication. He also wants to make sure that there are no side effects. He will call Dr. Schneider and see what needs to be done to make a conclusive diagnosis—Dr. Kerry warns that it may require a bone marrow sample, a skin biopsy, or a blood test be sent to a special lab in San Diego.

My parents are facing a difficult reality, both in terms of my physical condition and with regards to their pocketbook. Dr. Kerry seeks to assuage both of these worries.

"Jessica's situation is far from hopeless," he says, "and treating the Fanconi, as we are doing, will help preserve her kidneys. And even if she needs to go to a specialty clinic for treatment, the military will cover the cost."

We are grateful for the military system that we are in due to my father's Navy career, but my parents know that physicians are at the mercy of their commanding officers when it comes to hospital placement. Dr. Kerry assures us that he will remain at Letterman for another year.

My parents receive a phone call later that afternoon. Dr. Kerry has spoken with Dr. Schneider. He reports that there has been some success with an experimental drug designed to lower cystine levels. In some cases, the drug has reduced the cystine level in the white blood cells by ninety percent.

Unfortunately, there is no long-term data at this time. There are about eighty children in the experimental drug study, and side effects have been minimal—although Dr. Kerry emphasizes that the study has not been published yet and when it is, the side effects will be fully delineated. In addition to depleting cystine, the medication seems to increase the growth velocity, although the reasons are unclear. Dr. Kerry believes that the drug sounds safe, but he will look over the protocol carefully before we decide whether or not I should take it. My blood will be drawn again (it's no small wonder that I have any left!) and sent to Dr. Schneider after it undergoes a special processing procedure at UCSF Medical Center, since the Letterman lab is not equipped to conduct the test.

Getting me on the new drug will require special permission from the Army and a lot of paperwork. As with any bureaucratic process, it will take time. Dr. Kerry will start the ball rolling with some preliminary forms.

My parents are told that there is a doctor at UCSF who is not optimistic about the experimental drug and another family with a young child being seen at nearby Stanford Hospital that has opted not to take the medication.

At this time in 1983, though, treating renal tubular acidosis using vitamin D is also experimental, and I am finally starting to see some improvement in my bones. Perhaps I'll experience an analogous set of benefits from the new medication. As someone with cystinosis, my fate without treatment is known—and really, with that outcome in mind, what is there to lose?

It has been a month since I was first admitted to Letterman Army Medical Center. I have conclusive diagnoses of rickets and renal tubular acidosis due to Fanconi syndrome and a tentative diagnosis of infantile nephropathic cystinosis. My polycitra has been increased several times in an attempt to raise my electrolytes. Every day, my mom tediously takes a needle and syringe to a tiny vitamin D capsule, extracts the liquid contents, and puts this in my milk. My thirst is seemingly insatiable and I am drinking more than a quart of milk a day. My parents are told that they must never deny me water or milk, because my condition predisposes me to dehydration. I drink so much that my urine samples are colorless. I don't eat solid food, but the milk is considered helpful owing to its high calcium and phosphorus content.

Various options for increasing my caloric intake are discussed. My parents consider adding egg to milkshakes or trying a prescription sugar supplement to boost my calories. The potential of a nasal feeding tube looms over them as they try to whet my appetite for a heartier diet.

Meanwhile, I am begging my mom to take me roller skating again. She is worried about my rickets and overall fragility. She phones Dr. Kerry.

"Jessica wants to go roller skating," she tells him. "I am concerned about her bones."

Dr. Kerry's response is emphatic. "Take her. She needs the exercise and you all need to continue doing the things you enjoy. Treat her *normally.*"

"But what if she breaks a bone?"

"If she breaks a bone," he says, "we will deal with it."

I am overjoyed at the prospect of an imminent trip to the roller rink. It is, in more ways than one, just what the doctor ordered.

In general, I am happier. I don't feel as miserable and my parents notice that I am significantly less irritable. By the time of my June 15 appointment, I am starting to look a bit like my old self, and a quick measurement confirms that I have grown in height. Although treating the renal tubular acidosis might not be addressing the root cause of my illness, it is having a positive effect.

The blood to be sent to Dr. Schneider's lab in San Diego is finally drawn with special permission from the Army. It will measure cystine content in the white blood cells in order to confirm diagnosis. My parents experience a ray of hope when Dr. Kerry reports that there is a child being seen at UCSF Medical Center who has cystine in her eyes but not in her white cells.

My parents and doctors feel that I am well enough to take a family trip to Texas to see my grandparents, aunts, uncles, and cousins. The southern summer heat, though, proves to be too much for me. I am hospitalized on

July 9-11, 1983 at the Women's and Children's Hospital in Odessa, Texas. I am very dehydrated and require IV fluids for the duration of my stay. Despite unfamiliarity with my condition, I receive good care at the hands of an excellent physician while in Odessa. When we return to Letterman three days later on my second birthday, Dr. Kerry is pleased with how I was treated while in Texas.

It isn't the only good news we receive that day: Dr. Kerry tells us that there is a woman whose grandson has cystinosis, and she is starting a Cystinosis Foundation in Oakland. Oakland! My parents cannot believe God's providence. The disease is extremely rare, and yet a foundation is being started less than an hour away from our home at the precise time that I am diagnosed. My parents, with jaws practically on the floor, examine the invitation.

The Newly Formed
CYSTINOSIS FOUNDATION OF CALIFORNIA
Invites You To An Open House
To Greet
DR. JERRY SCHNEIDER
University of California Medical School
at
La Jolla, CA
and Colleagues
In the Field of Research and Treatment of Cystinosis
Thursday, July 28, 1983
5:30 – 7:30
Oakland, CA

Dr. Kerry says he plans to go to the meeting on July 28. My mom immediately commits to going as well.

It isn't until after meeting with other families and connecting with Dr. Schneider that my parents start to feel less alone. When my test results come in from San Diego, my mom is told that my white cell cystine level is 3.9. A healthy person's cystine level is a small fraction of 1. She calls one of the women she met at the Cystinosis Foundation Open House.

"Jessica's white cell cystine level is 3.9," she tells the other mother, who has an eleven-year-old with the disease.

"Gayle, our daughter's cystine level was 3.9 when she was eight years old and before she began the new experimental treatment."

The results are conclusive. I have infantile nephropathic cystinosis.

ruminations from the rink

It is perhaps ironic that one of history's most famous atheists asserted that *no victor believes in chance.* Taken out of context, this quotation can be easily applied to the circumstances surrounding the discovery of my cystinosis. There are a lot of miracles in my diagnosis story, and I have to marvel at the blessings I had showered upon me from the very beginning. The many coincidences that came at this time were, in fact, divine appointments. **In other words, the coincidences were predestined by a merciful God.**

Out of my family's most monumental problem in 1983 came a most incredible solution: we were able to connect with other families through the Cystinosis Foundation. That the Foundation was formed in the same year as my diagnosis and less than an hour away (when there were only 100-200 known cases of the disease spread throughout the entire country) seems to be a piece of conclusive evidence that God has always held my future securely in His hands. *No victor believes in chance.*

God also worked through the hands of my physicians. There are doctors who take the Hippocratic oath very seriously, and then there are doctors who consider "above and beyond" to be an irreplaceable part of their job description as carers for the sick. Dr. Kerry devoted countless hours to my case. He attended meetings and advocated on my behalf. He accompanied my mom to the Cystinosis Foundation Open House. His devotion took the hazardous unsolved mystery of my life and turned it not into a death sentence, but into a diagnosed condition to be treated.

The day I entered Dr. Kerry's office was not just an afternoon doctor consultation. It was a divine appointment and I emerged victorious. *No victor believes in chance.*

If there is anything I've learned over the years, it's that when these divine appointments present themselves, you don't reschedule. And to the victors go the roller rinks of former impossibility, ready for traversing at the speed of light.

Rolling forward…

three | it was the best of medicines, it was the worst of medicines

In any decision situation, the amount of relevant information available is inversely proportional to the importance of the decision.

Cooke's Law

There are some remedies worse than the disease.

Publilius Syrus

With my diagnosis confirmed, work begins to start me on cysteamine, the experimental drug being used by Dr. Schneider at UCSD to treat cystine accumulation in the cells.

Although my family might not know it at the time, this is an exciting development. In the early days of cystinosis research, there are no specific treatments to target the cystine. Addressing the disease symptomatically primarily involves replacing the electrolytes and other nutrients that are lost in the urine—and this is what my regimen has been up until this point. There is no doubt that a change is needed! The *Los Angeles Times* sums up the bleak prognosis of an untreated child in an article from 1986 featuring Dr. Schneider.

> *Schneider said that children who have the inherited problem appear normal at birth but develop signs of cystinosis within six to eight months, usually beginning with sugar in the urine, consumption of large amounts of water, and evidence of rickets.*
>
> *If not diagnosed properly or left untreated, children will die within a couple of years. Symptomatic treatment—continually replenishing water and salts—allows children to live several years, usually to age*

nine or ten, although growth is severely stunted. A six-year-old with the disease usually is no taller than a normal three-year-old.

I read statements such as these—rather conclusive assertions that seemingly reduce my years to ten—and I am enormously thankful for being born into a different era. Dr. Schneider, who first encountered cystinosis at the government-funded National Institutes of Health (NIH) in 1965, understood early that the cystine crystals are the key to the disease. Once he became involved with some of the families of children with cystinosis, they grabbed hold of him, drew him into their community, and wouldn't let him go. This isn't too hard to believe—one meeting with Dr. Schneider and you realize his compassion, his intelligence, his drive. I am very blessed to reap the benefits of his research. The article continues:

> *The conclusive evidence of cystine concentrations as the culprit opened the doors to research that Schneider has widened during the past two decades.*
>
> *About ten years ago, Schneider and his UCSD laboratory colleagues discovered that the drug cysteamine would dissolve the amino acid out of white cells.*
>
> *…The drug has been studied now to the point where any child diagnosed with the disease is eligible to receive it, either through an ongoing study at UCSD or through a parallel, but smaller, study at the National Institutes of Health in Washington.*

However, things are a bit different in 1983, three years before the *Los Angeles Times* piece is published. In October, Dr. Kerry calls my parents to let them know that Dr. Schneider is not officially accepting any additional patients into his study, but because of a verbal agreement made at the Cystinosis Foundation meeting in July, I am allowed to enroll. My cystine level of 3.9 is very high and time is of the essence. Dr. Kerry presents a timeline for obtaining the drug through Letterman Army Medical Center and starting treatment.

Dr. Schneider needs two or three more white blood cell evaluations before I start cysteamine, so I'll have another blood test at the beginning of November. Around the same time, Dr. Kerry will meet with the Committee on Investigative Studies at Letterman, at which point he will tell the panel about the experimental program at UCSD.

Once approval is granted, I will be admitted to the hospital in the first week of December and all blood tests will be repeated. Cysteamine will be started in low doses as I gradually work my way up to the maximum, 50 milligrams per kilogram of body weight per day. I will be closely monitored for side effects. Once the maximum dosage is reached, I will be readmitted to the hospital and the tests will be repeated.

The reality sinks in that it will take about two months to get me into the program. My parents are frustrated with the timetable, since they feel that I am already at least a year behind in terms of combating the cystine in my cells. At the same time, they struggle with the potential side effects that accompany the experimental drug: nausea, vomiting, dizziness, lethargy, and possibly some more serious ones.

Along with the unknowns, though, come many hard truths: I am still not on the growth chart, my blood tests are showing kidney damage, and I have a toxic amount of cystine in my body. My parents feel that it is time to plunge into the unproven but promising.

Once this decision is made, my mom feels rather helpless as she waits for approval for the cysteamine. She calls many doctors and puts pressure on them to speed the process up. The head of Pediatrics at Letterman, Dr. Brown, tells her that a few more weeks won't make a huge difference.

She laments this response. "But we're already a year behind!"

To compound my mother's frustration, there is only one lab—at UCSF Medical Center—in our area that will do the white blood cell separation required for the cystine test at UCSD. The lab only performs this process once a month, and due to paperwork lag time, I have missed the day in October and am unable to do another white blood cell cystine test until November 14. At that time, a doctor and two lab technicians approach their two-year-old patient with apprehension—but again, I sit still and merely watch with interest as three vials of blood are collected.

The Thanksgiving holiday approaches and I am still not on cysteamine. For about a week at the end of November, I vomit—forcibly—several times a day. Frustration mounts. My parents don't know what is causing my sudden illness, but they are more desperate for the cysteamine than ever. It is difficult enough knowing that I am sick—but to also realize that a promising treatment is out there is almost unbearable. Dr. Kerry calls to tell us that the commanding officer of Letterman must sign the orders for me to receive the drug, and the paperwork remains unsigned. I am certain that the commanding officer of a major military hospital is a very busy man, but knowing that doesn't make it any easier.

We are now told that I might start cysteamine the week before Christmas.

In reality, it is the second week of January 1984 that I am admitted to the hospital. January 8 is the last day that my parents will get a full night of sleep for fifteen years.

Cysteamine is a vile liquid that must be taken every six hours, around the clock. My starting dose is quite low, but I gag at the taste. I am kept in the hospital for two days for monitoring, but my body seems to tolerate the medication. My parents are once again warned of potential side effects, and then I am released. The medication is increased every twenty-one days until I reach the maximum dose for my size.

It is an exciting time to be cognizant of the positive changes in the cystinosis world, though of course, I am not. Unaware of the progress, I am nonetheless a beneficiary (and in some ways also a benefactor), a guinea pig, and a success story in this quest to improve the treatment of patients with the disease. Cysteamine truly represents a miracle drug and a lifeline, single-handedly extending our days on this earth by years certainly, decades probably—but it is all still unknown at this point.

What is evident from the very beginning is that this drug has its flaws, but in no uncertain terms should the champagne be thrown out with the cork. My parents are determined that I will stay on it. That being said, there are other families who drop out of the study, and it is hard to find fault with this decision either, as in the early- to mid-1980s it carries unspecified long-term benefits—though the short-term hardships are clearly communicated in the *Los Angeles Times* article.

While cysteamine has no serious side effects, it has "an incredibly bad taste and smells like rotten eggs," Schneider said. Furthermore, the drug must be taken every six hours indefinitely, he said. A new odorless and tasteless version of the drug is being presented for use later this year. Schneider hopes that if the new drug proves as effective, it will increase compliance among children.

"We have had between ten and fifteen percent of the children who started the study withdraw because of the terrible taste and smell," he said. "And we are not sure how many take it all the time."

Can *no serious side effects* and *terrible taste and smell* truly be reconciled? For any child growing up and trying to fit in, unpleasant body aroma— for cysteamine creates a sulfur-like smell that seems to seep through the pores—is a mighty conundrum with which to contend. Upon starting the drug in 1984, the odor almost immediately presents a problem for me. My parents are diligent about giving me the drug every six hours—at 7:30 a.m., 1:30 p.m., 7:30 p.m., and 1:30 a.m.—but they struggle to ride in the same car as me unless fresh air is allowed to flow freely through the interior. My mom networks with the small cystinosis community that she has connected with through her volunteer job as editor of the Cystinosis Foundation newsletter and learns that some parents have found success by brushing their children's teeth with baking soda and putting a little bit of the powder in the bathtub. Eager to try anything to combat the smell, my mom is relieved to discover that this strategy alleviates the situation somewhat.

Less than a year after my diagnosis, the cysteamine study and I are prominently featured in an article in the May 2, 1984 edition of the *San Francisco Examiner,* called *Aiding dying kids and their lonely parents.* The well-written piece, which focuses on one of the early research conferences held in San Francisco, does a remarkable job of capturing the dire outlook that my parents—and all parents of children with cystinosis—are presented with at this time, despite the potential of the new medicine.

The request came often and loudly: "Mommy, I want more water."

A half-dozen children, stricken with a rare disease called cystinosis, roamed around during an informal seminar on the illness yesterday at a pediatric research convention in San Francisco. They were like restless kids at any adult function, except for their frequent pleas for water.

I still cringe at the use of the word *stricken*. It sounds as though a lightning bolt has sent its electrifying—and fatal—power into me, its innocent victim. I don't feel that I have been stricken with anything, though I certainly count my blessings every day. The paper doesn't mince words, and Staff Writer Stephanie Salter doesn't sugarcoat.

The disease is fatal. As cystinotic children grow older, their kidneys deteriorate, and they require dialysis. Few of them live beyond their teens.

Jessica Britt of San Carlos typifies the few hundred American children with cystinosis. She is blond, fair, and looks like a healthy, rambunctious two-year-old—except she is nearly three. Her retarded physical growth is another aspect of the disease.

"She was a nine-pound baby, but in one year she didn't grow," said Jessica's mother, Gayle. "She went from the ninety-nine percentile on the growth scale to the minus-five percentile."

After relating the story of my diagnosis and the formation of the Cystinosis Foundation, the paper goes on to share the more personal side of my life with the disease and its treatment.

Along with some eighty other children in this country and Canada, Jessica is taking a new drug, cysteamine, which helps rid the body of excess cystine. A sulfur-based drug, cysteamine smells and tastes like rotten eggs, and many older children with cystinosis literally cannot stomach it.

"We feel blessed that she's not throwing it up," Mrs. Britt said. "Sometimes she'll balk because it stinks, but sometimes she'll say, 'I know, it's for my body.'"

The thought of a nearly three-year-old version of me telling my mom that I take cysteamine because I know it is good for my body is almost too much to take. Where is this knowledge eight and then fifteen years later, when I decide to pursue a life of noncompliance?

"But I know the most cysteamine will do is slow down (the disease)," *she said. "I still look at her sometimes and cry. People will say, 'Oh,* *you have such a beautiful daughter,' and I think, 'Yes, but she's dying.'"*

Yet, as so often happens to parents with terminally ill children, the *Britts have found positive elements in their tragedy. A religious family,* *they see whatever time they have with Jessica as a blessing.*

And they still hope.

"I know children go to heaven when they die," Mrs. Britt said, "but I *also know I want God to heal my daughter."*

At least temporarily, my mixture of cysteamine and polycitra seems to have the healing properties that my mom is praying for. Frequent blood tests reveal that the natural progression of the disease is indeed slowing. (Perhaps my *tragedy*, as the newspaper terms it, is being rewritten?) With every regular lab draw, my father graphs my creatinine level (a measure of kidney function) on immaculate, hand-rendered charts that are stacked neatly on the kitchen counter for all family members to see; for several years, this figure remains below one, indicating decent renal performance. My Fanconi syndrome is controlled through sodium, potassium, and bicarbonate supplementation, and regular trips to UCSD as part of the cysteamine study show that my white blood cell cystine level, while still much higher than that of a healthy individual, generally stays below one as well.

Dr. Kerry leaves Letterman for another assignment, and I am put under the care of a general pediatrician at the hospital. He monitors my growth (which is now running parallel to the normal growth curve, albeit at a position lower than the average range), orders my labs and experimental medication, and fills out frequent paperwork for the UCSD study. My cysteamine dose increases typically coincide with my white blood cell cystine level tests, done several times a year, and although these mean that more of the foul-tasting medication must be consumed, more medicine in my little plastic shot cup also indicates that I am outgrowing previous smaller amounts. And after the nightmare of my failure to thrive and diagnosis, growth can only be celebrated.

Two years after being put on the original liquid cysteamine, a new version of the drug carries with it the promise of being odorless and tasteless. In the November 3, 1986 edition of our local *San Mateo County Times-Tribune*, the excitement—and the apprehension—surrounding phosphocysteamine is perspicuous.

> *Meanwhile, a new drug called phosphocysteamine—a product that apparently is odorless and does not taste particularly bad—has been developed.*
>
> *Some parents are apprehensive. Britt worries because Jessica has done well on cysteamine and she is afraid of jeopardizing her progress and possibly her life.*
>
> *"It is an incredibly interesting predicament," said Schneider. "Half the parents are terrified to change because the children are doing so well. The other half are terrified that they won't be put on phosphocysteamine."*

After jumping through hoops and enduring another round of bureaucratic red tape at Letterman, our freezer is packed with the new experimental drug, which is really just a reformulated version of cysteamine. Unfortunately, though, the promises fall short: while odorless and tasteless in small quantities in a lab environment, where phosphates chemically overpower the sulfur, in large quantities the phosphate-sulfur bond proves to be unstable. I tolerate the phosphocysteamine fairly well—I am sometimes nauseous and I occasionally throw up, but it is a small price to pay for healthy cystine levels—but the smell still haunts me. Cysteamine is cysteamine.

Of course, it is nearly impossible to smell oneself, and at the ripe old age of five I am more interested in making my kindergarten teacher and parents proud than in odor management.

In fact, I am very rarely teased at school. There are a few good-natured comments about my size, and I am the victim of a non-politically correct policy common in the 1980s: lining up students by height when leaving the classroom for an assembly in the multipurpose room or organizing a seating chart. This policy leaves me at the head of the line and in the front row of the classroom, but surprisingly, there is a little boy in my grade who is, at times through the years, shorter than I am. I go through elementary school, then, feeling relatively normal, whereas his gender— with its accompanying bigger-and-stronger expectations—earns him some unfortunate labels relating to his height. The time between my morning and afternoon doses of cysteamine is spread to seven hours so that the drug doesn't have to be administered at school, and there is no mention of the odor by my classmates.

The silence is broken when I enter junior high. Once again I find myself in the front row of a classroom, this time in sixth grade Social Studies. With a new, third trimester seating chart, I am sitting next to a boy who makes up his lack in height with excess in humor; he is enormously popular and I quickly become enamored, feeling very fortunate to have him as my vertically challenged desk neighbor. By the third day of the new seating arrangement, though, he is wrinkling his nose.

"Do you smell that?" he asks me before focusing on his daily geography exercise. "It smells like rotten eggs!"

I don't smell anything, and I say so.

It happens two more times before he draws the obvious conclusion: the smell is coming from me.

I am mortified.

The next morning, I quickly pocket Cystagon—the new, still-experimental (but well on its way to government approval) capsule version of cysteamine that has replaced the phosphocysteamine and cysteamine liquids—and toss the pills on my way to the bus stop. I don't think this through, but I also don't feel any immediate negative consequences. The positive side effect, though, is evident—my neighbor is silent on the subject of odor.

I continue this practice for the remainder of sixth grade, though in the summer I am without my morning walks to the bus stop—and stroll by our condominium complex's garbage bin—so I take to hiding the pills in various places in the house. I very much live in the moment. It doesn't occur to me that eventually, I will either need to bag all the pills and take them to the dumpster, my room will start to smell so bad that my family will get suspicious, or my crime will be discovered. Because I have never felt sick, my scheme at first jives with how I see myself: normal. Only my unstable labs and subsequent medical appointments serve as a reminder that I am living with a progressive disease.

Even then, though, I still feel fine—perhaps my deterioration is so slow that I don't notice—so I continue down the path of noncompliance without garnering suspicion. As an added bonus, my typical morning nausea goes the way of the tossed Cystagon. What liquid cysteamine allowed was tiny dose increases; an adjustment as small as one-tenth of a milliliter was possible when my cystine level ran too high. But with the new pill form, the smallest dosage is a 50 milligram capsule. I therefore am put on a higher dose of cysteamine than before, and noncompliance offers some much-desired relief from my stomach's resultant protests.

Seventh grade begins and I am feeling confident, social, and healthy. However, a regular four-month white cell cystine level test, sent to UCSD, reveals that my numbers have increased significantly. Assuming it is an error, my doctor orders a repeat test. This time the result is even worse.

Perplexed, my mom calls Dr. Schneider. She wants to know why I am not absorbing the cysteamine. Has my body developed immunity to it? Do I need to take more? Dr. Schneider senses her concern and requests that we come to UCSD so that he can monitor my body's reaction to cysteamine in the hospital. The transition from liquid to capsule is still relatively new—and of course, no form of cysteamine is approved by the Food and Drug Administration despite its proven success in lowering intracellular cystine—and if there is a patient having problems with it, he wants to know.

I am worried. I know, of course, that I am to blame for my poor test results, but it still comes as a surprise. My twelve-year-old reasoning leads me to ponder how it is even possible that I am so sick when I feel the same as I always have. As our trip approaches, I start taking my Cystagon more diligently. I don't hear any comments about odor at school, but subconsciously I still question the necessity of the drug. Nevertheless, I am determined to pass Dr. Schneider's tests with flying colors.

The opportunity to prove my talents at faking blood test results never presents itself, though. (At least... not in this instance.) A few days before packing the car up and traveling 400 miles to San Diego, my parents discover my hidden stash of Cystagon. I am in serious trouble. Do I realize what I've done?

The sad truth is no, I don't.

My mom tearfully calls Dr. Schneider later that night to reveal my transgression. They come to a consensus that with this new information, the trip to UCSD is unnecessary. Dr. Schneider is sympathetic, but firm—two attributes that make him an excellent doctor.

"Unfortunately, it happens," he tells her. "You see, in a person with diabetes, the effects of noncompliance are immediately felt. The patient feels worse if he skips his medication and will, more than likely, resume taking it fairly soon. In the case of someone with cystinosis, there are no immediate side effects of not taking Cystagon. And it is hard for an adolescent to understand that it is so necessary to be compliant."

He is right, of course. In fact, I feel *better* without taking Cystagon—something that holds true in my thirties as much as it does when I am twelve—due to the drug's propensity to cause nausea and other gastrointestinal problems. Nevertheless, when I am under my parents' roof, noncompliance is not an option. Moving forward, my parents closely monitor me as I take my medication, watching as every last Cystagon pill and drop of liquid polycitra are swallowed. They know that this medication is my lifeline, and that with nearly a year of sporadic consumption, I have done unknown damage.

The damage soon becomes known. I have propelled myself into kidney failure, and by the time I am a sophomore in high school my physicians are discussing dialysis and transplant. While I cannot be sure that strict cysteamine compliance would have postponed this need for many years, I feel certain that I could have at least completed high school without entering the tumultuous waters of end-stage renal disease.

ruminations from the rink

I was born right around the time that there was a significant turning point in the treatment of cystinosis. Rather than just be treated symptomatically as problems—such as electrolyte depletion, hypothyroidism, and kidney failure—arose, I had the opportunity to receive a drug that actually addressed the root cause, excess cystine.

The first experiments with cysteamine as a treatment for cystinosis were conducted in 1977, a mere four years before my birth. Other experimental treatments for cystinosis—including penicillamine, a low-cystine diet, and high doses of vitamin C—had all proven ineffective at best, detrimental at worst. Cysteamine was the first product able to effectively eliminate cystine from the cells. This conclusive information was not fully known at the time of my diagnosis, and my parents had to make a very difficult decision with not a whole lot of data.

Thankfully, they made the right choice by putting me on the medicine. Whatever its form—cysteamine, phosphocysteamine, or finally, a pill branded under the Cystagon name—this drug literally saves lives. It extends the estimated lifespan of a person with cystinosis by decades. It is not a cure, but it is the next best thing.

And yet, it is vile. More than just having a terrible taste and smell, it can often make its patient feel as though her stomach is aflame. When I made the painful decision to reintroduce Cystagon into my life after many adult years of noncompliance (more on this later), I experienced the side effects full throttle. The drug takes away my appetite and yet is impossible to tolerate on an empty stomach. It addresses a key metabolic problem and yet causes tremendous lethargy. It saves my life but at times eats away at my ability to live it to the fullest, making me shy away from getting close to people for fear that they might get a whiff of its hideous odor. How's that for a set of discouraging Catch-22s?

My husband, in an effort to understand my complaints about cysteamine, once committed to taking Cystagon for a period of three days. He got through two before saying, "I feel like I have a sulfur balloon in my stomach. If this is supposed to make you better, then I don't want to know what worse feels like."

I cannot be more clear, though: in the case of Cystagon and cystinosis, the remedy (imperfect as it is) is *not* worse than the disease, though at times it certainly feels that way. Could I have permanently learned the lesson that I apparently knew when I was three—that cysteamine is good for my body—and applied it to life at age twelve or while in my twenties, I would more than likely not be contemplating my own mortality at the age of thirty.

The paradox, then, is obvious. **Like any dieter knows, sometimes what is best for us to consume can be the most difficult to stomach.** More than that, though, medicine can also hurt. In the case of cystinosis, our lifeline can both increase the quantity and deteriorate the quality of our days.

What actions are you taking now that your body—or your soul—will thank you for in the future? What are you putting off until you feel you *really need it?* Is it possible that you need a little discomfort now in order to truly thrive?

Most importantly, remember this: Whatever mistakes you have made in your past, regrets are not what will reverse them. My medical redemption comes from altering my future based on what I have finally learned from what the three-year-old Jessica Britt had to say. Never again do I want to take for granted the era in which I was born—the cysteamine era. My forerunners with cystinosis were less fortunate when it came to treatment options, but I am given a choice.

What medicine do you need to start taking?

Rolling forward…

four | social networking without facebook

Always remember that you are absolutely unique.
Just like everyone else.

Margaret Mead

A brief history of Internet social networking: The United States Department of Defense develops the Advanced Research Projects Agency Network (ARPANET) in the 1960s as a way to communicate and link various research centers. This concept later evolves into the Internet and the World Wide Web, a civilian-friendly network of documents and pages containing useful, erroneous, and offensive information alike. In 2002, Friendster is launched and is followed shortly thereafter by MySpace; in 2004, Facebook makes its debut on the Web and soon grows to become the largest social networking site linking friends, old flames, and strangers obsessed with watering imaginary crops and buying imaginary cows in an imaginary land.

Despite all its flaws, social networking provides one of the easiest ways for people within rare disease communities to connect. Individuals who once felt so alone find that there are others with which they can identify. A disease such as cystinosis, which affects a few thousand people worldwide, becomes a common topic of discussion within certain Facebook groups.

(A brief history of human social networking: Eve said to the serpent, *let me go tell my husband about this awesome fruit so that he too can update his status as one now knowledgeable about good and evil.*)

Immediately following my diagnosis in 1983, my parents feel very alone. Upon finding the Cystinosis Foundation, they realize that there are others like me scattered around the country. There is no home Internet, and air travel to visit others in the cystinosis community, however appealing, is impractical. So mothers and fathers pick up their pens or take to their typewriters and begin to write round robin letters to one another.

My mom writes my story and sends it to the next person in a chain of six. The recipient reads my family's letter, writes one for her own child, and sends both letters to the next person in the chain. When the letters make their way back to my mom, she copies all the stories and distributes them to people in her chain and other chains that have been running simultaneously.

Each story that comes in is remarkably similar, yet monotony does not set in when my parents read them. There are multiple accounts of family doctors who, convinced that the overprotective mother is the one at fault, seek to assure parents that nothing is wrong with their child. There are mothers who are called *enablers* for letting their children drink as much water as they desire, thus sabotaging their appetites and ushering in a failure to thrive.

Before a correct diagnosis but after the onset of symptoms, many children with cystinosis struggle to keep anything remotely caloric in their stomachs, they lose weight, they drink water anywhere they can find it (including bath tubs, pet dishes, and outside sprinklers), they walk (and sleep) with constantly wet diapers, and they are misdiagnosed with diabetes due to sugar in the urine and excessive thirst. Many initially have rickets and struggle to reach those all-important baby milestones of crawling, walking, and running.

Letter after letter, though, has an upbeat tone in light of diagnosis (via slit lamp, skin biopsy, white blood cell cystine level, or bone marrow test) and treatment. Many experience a dramatic change simply with the addition of polycitra, an alkalizer designed to replace depleted potassium and sodium and metabolize into bicarbonate. At least half of the round robins that come in speak to the remarkable change in appetite after starting cysteamine. Of course, the unique food preferences are often mentioned—pickles, salt and vinegar potato chips, processed deli meats, and any tomato-based sauce seem to be particular favorites of children unconsciously making an effort to replace the salt their bodies cannot hold onto—and celebrated as a complete 180-degree turn from the time when food held no interest and growth stagnated.

My mother's round robin letter feels to her like a retelling of the same story with the names changed. However, her letter shares a unique and specific-to-us narrative that surely resonates with other mothers who are all too familiar with the general sequence: initially healthy baby, eventual failure to thrive, diagnosis, and attempts to achieve normalcy.

December 3, 1983

Dear Friends,

This is the first of a round robin letter. When you get this letter, add yours to it and send to the next person on the enclosed list. The last person will send all the letters back to me and I will send them to you. That way we will all get to read all the letters. Since cystinosis involves so few, it is nice that we can exchange information in this way. In fact, I just had Jessica in to the doctor this week and asked him a question about her diet. He said that the best source of information about diet is from parents who have experienced the feeding problems unique to the disease. In many ways I feel that my story is the same as yours and that only the names are different. But, let me begin.

Our second daughter, Jessica, was born July 14, 1981, a beautiful, healthy, nine-pound baby. We took her for her regular baby checkups (two weeks, two months, seven months at our clinic) and everything was fine. But by about one year of age she wasn't walking and was generally inactive. She wanted to be carried everywhere. I attributed all this to her sweet, loving disposition. At her one-year checkup she had not grown a bit or gained a pound since the previous checkup at seven months. She had gone from the ninety-ninth percentile to a minus-five percentile on the growth chart. This alerted the doctors and we were asked to bring her back every few months. She began walking at seventeen months and at eighteen months she had grown a little but still didn't make the curve on the growth chart. At twenty-one months she was placed in the hospital for tests and at almost twenty-two months she was finally diagnosed. The doctor explained that she had rickets and renal tubular acidosis (Fanconi syndrome) and that he would be treating these conditions but that there was no treatment or cure for cystinosis.

(I wrote this in condensed form and didn't go into the details of those months and different doctors. I took Jessica in for an ear infection and had to see a doctor we had never seen before and he took one look at her growth chart and started the wheels rolling toward a diagnosis. I also didn't mention that after she was diagnosed with Fanconi we were sent to an ophthalmologist who did not bother to look at her eyes under a slit lamp even though the pediatrician requested so. I didn't know what a slit lamp was then so I accepted what he said. We were told that she did NOT have cystinosis. But our pediatrician decided to have an ophthalmologist look again. Before that my husband and I went to the library and looked up cystinosis in a medical dictionary. So when we took Jessa to the second ophthalmologist, I told him that I wanted to know if there were any cystine crystals in her eyes. When he told me there were and called in three other doctors to look (including the doctor who hadn't looked before), I knew the diagnosis. So before the pediatrician told us, we knew all about cystinosis.)

The emotional turmoil that we went through was greatly lightened by the prayers of our family and friends. We know God's hand is in all this.

Jessica was put on Rocaltrol, which is a vitamin D supplement, and polycitra. Since we started the polycitra Jessica stopped eating solid food. All she does is drink. Fortunately she loves milk and we manage to get a quart down her a day. She also drinks her polycitra mixed with sixteen ounces of apple juice each day. And she drinks lots of water. She often looks bloated. She is growing bit by bit.

In July I took Jessica and her older sister to Texas to visit my parents. Her older sister caught a virus and passed it to Jessa. Jessa vomited and all but stopped drinking. She dehydrated so fast and so far that she was hospitalized and on IVs for two days to build her back up.

In August Jessa's blood sample was sent to Dr. Schneider at UCSD. It showed a cystine level of 3.9. The test was repeated in November and we are waiting for those results now. We plan to start Jessa on the experimental drug, cysteamine, soon.

Jessa's six-year-old sister, Kirsten, has been checked by an ophthalmologist and no cystine crystals were found in her eyes. Jessa's illness has affected Kirsten because of the amount of time and attention we must give Jessa. The two girls love each other dearly and play quite well together considering the four years between their ages. Jessica seems so normal and healthy that it is hard for Kirsten to understand she is sick. Recently, though, Jessa had the flu and Kirsten really rallied around her trying to entertain her, etc. The concern Kirsten showed in her face and in her prayers said it all.

Water is a very important part of Jessa's life. I got her a Hello Kitty thermos-type canteen that I put in her bed every night. (She also carries that canteen to church, shopping, the park, and everywhere!) We have watched her in her pretend play. She always puts her dolly "night, night" with a container of pretend water at dolly's side.

Jessa's diet consists of no solid foods (we offer them, but she very seldom even takes one bite), one quart of milk daily, and sixteen ounces of apple juice.

My husband and I are so pleased to be a part of the round robins. We feel it helpful to exchange information, and a need is fulfilled by being able to "talk" to those who are experiencing the same things we are. I hope that we can meet you some day.

Round robins exchanged a few months later see my mom adding information about my newest medication, cysteamine, and also an interesting subject that other parents are starting to bring up as well: the fact that cystinosis is an invisible illness.

In January 1984 we started Jessa on cysteamine. For the first three weeks the dose was 0.6 cc four times a day. Then it was doubled three weeks later, and again three weeks after that. She now takes 3.6 cc four times a day. We put it in her polycitra and tell her it is medicine that she must drink. We have never bribed her, but have just said matter-of-factly that she must drink it for her body. She sometimes pulls a stubborn act of refusing it, but so far she has always changed her mind and taken it. And now even the 1:30 a.m. dose is automatic.

Jessa has only thrown up the medicine once and that was when she was taken for a ride in the car immediately after taking the medicine. She has sometimes complained of a stomachache after taking the medicine, but it passes after a while. She is growing and is generally doing well. She is very, very pale and often awakens with bags under her eyes. But most people would not know that she is sick. She seems to eat a little better now. She still drinks at least a quart of milk a day and sometimes will eat a few grapes, or a piece of an apple, or a bite of pizza, or two bites of a Big Mac. Her favorite is bread and butter. She might even eat a whole piece of bread if it has a lot of butter on it. She doesn't care much for sweets, and somehow has been made to feel different because of it. Yesterday she came home from preschool and said excitedly to me that she had eaten a cookie. Jessa is in preschool two mornings a week for two hours each morning. She loves it and has no problems at all.

The improvement that cysteamine offers is palatable. Not only are there several letters in which parents emphatically state that appetites and growth have increased dramatically after cysteamine, but there are also families with multiple children with cystinosis—and in three such cases, one or more of those children died very young from the disease before the current son or daughter was even been a blip on the ultrasound. For these parents with a living child reaping the benefits of cysteamine, they know first-hand how much more devastating the disease was in the 1960s and 1970s.

The most heartbreaking letters come from parents of older children. Transplants are such an ordeal in the early 1980s, and post-transplant complications affect several of the older children with cystinosis. A few years later when we hear—not through the Internet, of course, but once again through the written word—about the death of a boy who recently had his transplant and was a playmate of mine at the most recent conference, our family takes the news very hard.

Nevertheless, the simple act of sharing experience—good or bad—provides intense solace for both the reader and the writer. In fact, there is so much comfort to be had in reading another child's diagnosis story that the round robins are expanded and repeated over the next couple years. The first cystinosis social networking group, started the year before Facebook founder Mark Zuckerberg's birth, is a success.

ruminations from the rink

The rare disease experience can be one of the loneliest in the world. Despite the theoretical knowledge that there were perhaps a couple thousand cases worldwide, before the round robin letters were started my parents had only met three children with cystinosis. The letters provided the opportunity for families to tune out the world of healthy children and immerse themselves in the words of others just like them.

Individually, we are few. But once we communicate, we become strong despite our small number—and we are no longer alone. **Though we are all absolutely unique, we have so much in common.** With these commonalities come consolation.

What are you experiencing in your life that leaves you feeling alone? Loneliness can bring sadness, fear, and hopelessness. While there is no one precisely like you, there are others who are going through similar circumstances, emotions, or addictions. God knows this and God wants you to know this—hence the words of the Psalmist, "God places the lonely in families, he sets the prisoners free and gives them joy" (Psalm 68:6 NLT). Not only have I grown to find great comfort in my placement in the worldwide cystinosis family, but I also know that I need not be a prisoner to loneliness or disease. I can go forth with joy and network with others who need to claim their freedom and their family as well.

Never lose hope that there is someone out there who wants to read your story, as well as a God who already knows it. Remember that Jesus himself knew pain and loneliness and cried out to God. And hold the words of Jesus dear: "And surely I am with you always, to the very end of the age" (Matthew 28:20).

Rolling forward…

five | catastrophic blessings and the accurate media

The extent of the catastrophe... gives the measure of the transformation that will be necessary in order to master it.

Lewis Mumford

Although it lacks the notoriety of cancer or heart disease, cystinosis is a killer, and all its victims are children.

David Martindale

Health, August 1982

There is a journalist sitting in our living room. She is asking me about cystinosis and my recent experience as a Wish recipient from the Make-A-Wish Foundation. I am silently wondering if she expects me to feel sorry for myself. It is only recently that I realized that self-pity is an emotion that many in the chronic disease community take on; I am suddenly very aware of my lack.

She seems to want to know how I am able to get up each morning, which puzzles me. Why wouldn't I get up? I tell her that my own optimism and my family's faith in God energize me.

Considering that we are part of such a small rare disease community, we do get a fair share of publicity in an effort to raise awareness about cystinosis. As soon as I am diagnosed, my parents begin collecting newspaper clippings that mention my condition. This tendency to archive information also works well with my mom's volunteer role as editor of the Cystinosis Foundation newsletter.

Articles about cystinosis often paint a picture that is extremely bleak. There are *fatal genes* that result in children *suffering from the disease* and lead parents to deal with the reality that they will have to *watch their children die*. While there may be half-truths or even truths in these statements, other articles contain blatant inaccuracies. In one article, I am described as a *victim of cystinosis,* something far from valid. Another piece states that ninety-nine percent of those with cystinosis have blond hair and blue eyes. One almost has to wonder if such statistics are simply fabricated in an effort to entice readers.

Nevertheless, people with the disease are certainly particular, both in the press and in reality. A Texas newspaper captures the fears of my grandparents in light of my diagnosis.

> *Elvia and Norma Gene Reynolds of Pecos have a unique granddaughter.*
>
> *But two-year-old Jessica Britt is unique not only to her grandfather and grandmother; she has also been the subject of research by many international doctors.*
>
> *Jessica is one of only a few hundred American children who have been diagnosed as having cystinosis, a disease that deteriorates kidneys and has killed most children it afflicts before they reach age ten.*
>
> *"A seven-year-old died with it last week—that really shook Gayle up," Mrs. Reynolds said of her daughter, Jessica's mother.*
>
> *Gayle and Ernest Britt of San Francisco noticed Jessica had stopped growing when she was nine months old. At a year old, she could not walk; x-rays showed the bones in her legs as only shadows.*
>
> *Jessica quit eating. She only wanted to drink water—and gallons of it at a time.*
>
> *"These children drink water like an alcoholic drinks," Mrs. Reynolds said. "They need it; they have got to have it."*

My grandmother is participating in fundraising efforts for the Cystinosis Foundation. The article has a dramatic finish, appropriate for a readership undoubtedly riveted by the poor child and the tragic headline—*Disease leaves family fighting time, death.*

"I'm real proud of all these people who have given," Mrs. Reynolds said. "Me—I have a special interest because of Jessica," she added.

"But even if she doesn't make it," Mrs. Reynolds concluded, "think of all the other children that could be helped."

And no doubt she is thinking about all the other children. Because that's just who my grandma is. Even at the age of two, I know this in my little heart.

In fact, many of my extended family members join in the effort to raise money for cystinosis research. In addition to the relatives who write letters to their Congressional representatives on my behalf in an attempt to increase government funding, my uncle in New Mexico spearheads a three-wheel rodeo fundraiser in December 1984. The rodeo, sponsored in part by Pecos Valley King's Kids (a division of the Christian Motorcyclists Association), is a success. My uncle emotionally pens in a letter to my mother, "I like to think of it as the same idea that I perceive you had and still have of caring and trying to use what you might have to improve somebody's life or chance to live."

I think these pieces of personal communication are more powerfully accurate than any newspaper or television account. My mom writes to Pecos Valley King's Kids after the event, "Jessica has richly blessed our lives for ever how long we have her. But God might just allow researchers to find a treatment that prolongs her life and the lives of other children and future children with the disease. You have contributed to that research. And, God willing, if not in time for Jessica, someday an effective treatment will be found."

Someday feels far off when I start kindergarten. As the months march on, we only see small glimpses of what is coming—and above all, we take it one day at a time. The beginning of school brings new challenges, touched upon on November 3, 1986 by the *San Mateo County Times-Tribune* article dramatically titled *Coping with cystinosis: Living with a rare catastrophic disease.*

> *Five-year-old Jessica had been in kindergarten just a week when her teacher phoned.*
>
> *"What are we going to do about Jessica and the water fountain?" she gently asked the child's mother, Gayle Britt of San Carlos.*
>
> *Jessica has a rare disease called cystinosis. In one day she will drink about a gallon of water and more than three quarts of milk. She eats practically no solid food.*
>
> *So great is her thirst and attraction to water that she will suck the water from her wash cloth if not restrained by her parents.*

Regardless of the disease's implications in general, for my part, I can think of far more catastrophic situations than spending too much time at the water fountain. But in describing this particular scenario, the article is fairly accurate.

One of the common features of children with cystinosis is excessive thirst and the need for water. When the cystine crystals build up in the renal tubular cells and damage them, it causes a loss of water due to an inability to conserve it within the body. Any fluid intake, therefore, tends to travel right through the child, who will excessively urinate no matter how much he drinks. The following helpful diagram appeared in the *Parents' Guide to Cystinosis,* produced by the National Institutes of Health for the U.S. Department of Health and Human Services in 1981. This diagram, which leaves me eternally thinking of my original kidneys as tanks without valves, clearly illustrates how important it is that neither my parents nor my kindergarten teacher deny me water: dehydration can come quickly and severely in a child with cystinosis.

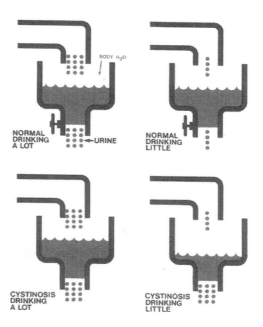

In addition to this unique aspect of the disease, the *Times-Tribune* article also focuses on my mother's reactions to her months-long search for a diagnosis and subsequent experience raising a chronically ill child.

> *The doctor suggested tests for cystinosis, but told the parents she probably did not have it.*
>
> *"I said, 'Well, at least she is not dying—is she?'" Britt recalled. "The doctor did not answer me."*
>
> *The Britts went to the library and pored over material on cystinosis. They read that cystine crystals are visible in the eyes of children with cystinosis. And they read that the children died by age ten.*
>
> *Britt was apprehensive as her anesthetized child slept during an eye examination. Finally she could stand it no more.*
>
> *"All I want to know is are there crystals?" she asked the ophthalmologist.*

"He said, 'Yes.' That was when I went to pieces."

At first the Britts struggled with just daily living—a struggle parents of catastrophically ill children know well. A religious woman, Britt could not look at the child they still regard today as "a blessing" without crying.

If Jessica was naughty, Britt told herself she could not spank a child who might die. And if Jessica left her toys scattered about, she asked Jessica's nine-year-old sister, Kirsten, to pick them up.

(I have an amazing sister. And, for "a blessing" being placed in quotation marks, I think I should make a submission to The "Blog" of "Unnecessary" Quotation Marks. But I digress.)

Slowly, she adjusted to more normal living with Jessica. Jessica made it easier because of her cheerful personality and her stoic manner of accepting discomfort.

I like the generally upbeat attitude of this article, despite some hard realities and frequent use of the word *sufferer* (I am certainly not one of those). Most importantly, I think the interviewer captures my personality.

As for Jessica, she is playful and happy, despite a low energy level.

On her first day in kindergarten, she told her mother in no uncertain terms that life was not keeping pace with her expectations.

"You were wrong, mother," she said as she came home. "They didn't teach me to read today."

The caption belonging to the article's accompanying photo—one of me playing the organ—says simply, "Despite having cystinosis, Jessica has a zest for life."

I am appreciative for the reporter for noticing. Indeed, in these early years, it is not always the case. In fact, an article from the *San Diego Union* that comes out the same year so eloquently (and erroneously) states that the disease will perpetually define my life.

> *One of the knowns is that because of kidney damage that has already started, children will never have a normal life. To expect any of them to have a normally full and complete life would be overly optimistic.*

Still, in the mid-1980s, some media reports suggest a changing of the tide. At least, as one article points out, patients are starting to live longer.

> *When he first began researching the disease back in 1965, said Schneider, all of those stricken with cystinosis died before the age of ten. Now, with the help of the new drug, some of the patients—who would have died—are now in their twenties. The drug, however, is not the cure, said Schneider. He said many of those patients who are in their twenties are now having problems with other organs, including loss of eyesight and neurological problems.*

Despite the unknowns of the future, I may live to see my eighteenth birthday—and legal adulthood—after all. Perhaps not all victims of cystinosis are children, and some of us may even grow to resist the victimhood so often applied to us.

On July 31, 1999, two weeks after my eighteenth birthday, the article about my Make-A-Wish experience comes out in the local newspaper. I am dismayed to see that the word *suffers* has once again been applied to my condition.

> *Jessica suffers from a rare disease, nephropathic cystinosis, that attacks the kidneys and other organs and is usually fatal before age thirty.*

What is it with doctors and the media all wanting to giving me an expiration date?

But her disease, dialysis, and seven operations haven't held her back so far. Jessica graduated with honors from Carlmont High in June, and plans on attending the University of California, Berkeley, in the fall to major in Electrical Engineering and Computer Science.

Hence, her wish: a computer store shopping spree that will begin Saturday with a limo ride to San Francisco, where Jessica, her mom, and her sister will get to eat lunch anywhere and shop for four hours.

Jessica said she was excited about the spree and happy about finding out about the group, which contacted her last month.

"I think it's so great to give kids that have so much hardship in life something they'll remember forever," she said. "And it's helpful to have a place to talk about your experiences."

The Foundation serves thirty to forty kids in the county each year. Wishes are donated by everyone from national corporations to local police departments.

Despite frequent nausea, fatigue, and undergoing multiple surgeries, Jessica participated in cheerleading in high school and has designed Web sites for the San Carlos School District, her mom, and a glass business in Sonoma.

In fact, after one of Jessica's surgeries, her mom said Jessica woke up in the hospital insisting on attending her calculus class.

"I think the doctors admired that kind of spirit," she said.

Jessica, who is on the waiting list for a kidney transplant, said her family's optimism and their faith in God keep her going.

Despite some small inaccuracies, the article ends on what I will later realize is one of my life's great truths—my own joy necessitates faith in God.

ruminations from the rink

In her bestselling book *The Happiness Project,* Gretchen Rubin makes a keen observation: there is something to be gained from reading of another person's challenges. Far from *schadenfreude* in nature, though, the reward stems more from the vicarious lessons to be learned. "I started by collecting accounts by people grappling with serious illness and death, but then I broadened my search to include any kind of catastrophe: divorce, paralysis, addiction, and all the rest. I hoped that it would be possible for me to benefit from the knowledge that these people had won with so much pain, without undergoing the same ordeals. There are some kinds of profound wisdom that I hope to never gain from my own experience" (p. 196).

It is for this reason—a desire to glean lessons from another's hardship—that I think many of the articles regarding cystinosis were, and continue to be, so bleak. It makes for a good story, but ultimately, life is what we make of it. Perhaps I was (and am) *catastrophically ill,* requiring countless hours of my parents' (and now my own and my husband's) time for administering medication, driving to doctors' appointments and dialysis, and sitting in hospital waiting rooms during surgeries. But I have also been labeled as *a blessing.* **And in sharing my own catastrophes, through the media or this memoir, my testimony can actually bless others, just as Rubin asserts.** What a glorious paradox!

Of course, my catastrophe would have ended up quite differently without the medications I was put on starting at an early age. As the 1984 Texas article pointed out, "The drugs have helped Jessica... so she can even roller skate, now her favorite pastime." For these drugs, I thank both the researchers involved in their development and a significant piece of legislation, as you will learn in the following chapter.

Rolling forward...

six | I am my parents' orphan

I am thirsty all the time.

At restaurants, I drink not only my own water, but everyone else's as well. When I sit in the bathtub, I occasionally drink directly out of the faucet and often suck the water out of my wash cloth. Middle-of-the-night medication doses are accompanied by the guzzling of vast quantities of water from the tap. My thirst is almost never quenched, and I am unable to see a water fountain without going to it for a drink. The excess cystine in my body is depositing in the tubular cells of my kidneys and damaging these cells; since the tubules aid in the reabsorption of water, it is easy to understand why my body is not conserving it at a normal rate. As Dr. Jess Thoene states in the Spring 1984 issue of *Generics,* my condition predisposes me to "life-threatening episodes of dehydration" which can be avoided "by allowing ad lib access to fluids and salty foods."

Although food isn't of terrible interest to me, my calorie needs are relatively fulfilled owing to the fact that I drown myself in nearly a gallon of milk each day. In second grade, I take a thermos of milk to school for lunch, but I am already aware that my behavior is not normal. I tell some of my classmates that the thermos contains soup. (I've heard of a challenge—apparently popular in some college circles—to drink a gallon of milk in an hour without vomiting. While I have no desire to take this challenge, if anyone can do it, it is probably my seven-year-old self, but unlike those fraternity brothers who enjoy the notoriety, I am not proud of my talent.) By third grade, I am taking a can of soda instead—but it is for keeping up appearances only. It generally ends up in a trash can or in the hands of a classmate before the school day is through. Most treats enjoyed by children my age are simply too sweet for my liking. My body craves the salt and fluid that it has so much trouble holding onto on its own.

Outside of social concerns, though, I enjoy the uniqueness that comes with having cystinosis. It sets a person apart, almost like being the smallest girl on the cheerleading squad secures one's destiny as the cheerleader chosen to be thrown in the air and put atop shoulders during stunts. (When I participate in cheerleading in high school, cystinosis ensures that I am the smallest member of the squad but also makes me unable to be the flyer due to concerns over kidney injuries. The injustice isn't lost on me.)

Rarity, however, is not without its pitfalls. Cysteamine, the only medication proven effective in removing cystine from the cells of a person with cystinosis, is labeled in 1982 by *Health* magazine as one of "the drugs nobody will make."

There is a legitimate reason for this that makes sense economically, though not necessarily morally. The United States is plagued with bureaucratic systems that sometimes serve dual blessing/curse functions; the Food and Drug Administration (FDA) is one such example. Getting new medications on the market is relatively easy in the early 1960s. Then comes a tragedy that points to the very real need for change: a number of expectant women take the drug thalidomide to alleviate the discomfort of morning sickness. The knowledge that this medication is harmful to the fetus is discovered far too late; thousands of babies develop birth deformities as a result. In response, Congress decides to impose new regulations for the approval of novel treatments; drugs must now pass more thorough clinical trials before being deemed acceptable for the market by the FDA.

I greatly appreciate that we have a vetting system for new drugs. I cringe at the thought of being allowed to take any substance for which a pharmaceutical company feels there is a market; the startling frequency with which patients demand antibiotics for viruses (instead of the bacterial conditions that antibiotics can treat) is indicative of just how eager we are to medicate.

Unfortunately, though, with the passage of these new policies in 1962, drug manufacturing becomes exponentially more expensive. With the number and scope of clinical trials now required, the conception-to-pharmacy development of a new treatment can cost millions of dollars—if not more. No doubt it is worth the cost if an effective treatment for cancer or diabetes is found. But what about cystinosis?

In 1982, *Health* magazine reports 100 known cases of cystinosis in the United States. Whether this number is entirely accurate or not, there is no doubt that there are certainly no more than double that number of diagnosed patients in the country at this time. (I am part of such an elite group!) Cysteamine, though tested for a few years at this point, is an "orphan drug" due to the small number of people who will be taking it. (In the cystinosis community, we are often "orphaned"—or overlooked—by major companies and organizations that might otherwise be able to help us.) There are a couple problems with orphan drug manufacturing in 1982: firstly, it is unlikely that such a drug will make a profit for a pharmaceutical company, as the number of customer-patients is so small and the development costs so high. Secondly, new FDA guidelines since the thalidomide debacle require that drug trials draw data from a large number—a few thousand—of clinical guinea pigs. With a disease affecting hundreds, where exactly would 3,000 test subjects come from?

This conundrum leads *Health* magazine article writer David Martindale to the obvious conclusion: "Yet despite the bright promise of cysteamine, no American drug manufacturer is interested in rigorously testing it to get it approved by the U.S. Food and Drug Administration."

And what of international attempts to market the drug? After all, intravenous cysteamine is, at this point, already used in the United Kingdom as an antidote for emergency-room cases of Tylenol overdose. (And, as an aside, it has also been studied by the U.S. Army for its radioprotective properties.) But living within the borders of a hegemonic superpower often means that your country's policies are either emulated or deferred to. While many other countries don't exactly have an equivalent of the FDA, they look to the U.S. standard to see if a proposed drug is safe. And with even fewer cystinosis cases than the U.S., the U.K. isn't in any immediate rush to manufacture cysteamine for home use, either.

Each individual rare disease might have few people affected by it, but when a united voice is formed from those impacted by all such diseases, the protest becomes vociferous and cankerous. A breakthrough occurs on January 4, 1983—about four months before I am diagnosed with the disease that I have already unknowingly lived with for a year and a half—when the Orphan Drug Act (ODA) is signed into law by President Ronald Reagan. Orphan drugs are generally defined as those medications with research and development costs much higher than expected profit returns. This piece of legislation offers pharmaceutical companies some incentives in developing orphan drugs: grants, tax breaks, expedited FDA application processing, and seven-year exclusivity on the market are just a few. The number of authorized medications for people with rare diseases increases sixfold over the next twenty years, as compared to the scarcity of the previous two decades.

Later that year, another bill is up for consideration: the National Institutes of Health Reauthorization Bill, also known as the Health Research Extension Act. In September 1983, my parents eagerly contact Representative Tom Lantos (D-CA), a proponent of the ODA, to encourage him to continue his support for the rare disease community. The emotions channeled into that meticulously typewritten letter are raw from my new diagnosis, but tactfully subdued.

Dear Congressman Lantos:

We want to thank you profoundly for your support of HR 2350, the NIH Reauthorization Bill, which contains provisions for the National Commission on Orphan Diseases.

Our two-year-old daughter has a rare genetic disease called cystinosis. At present there is no cure and no treatment for cystinosis, but an experimental drug is being tested. Because the disease is rare, drug companies are not too interested in making drugs to treat it. That is why the Orphan Drug Act was so important to us. We also need a National Commission on Orphan Diseases as contained in HR 2350. The work this Commission will do will benefit our daughter, Jessica, and hundreds like her who do not have common diseases, yet have no less fatal ones.

To further emphasize our support, we attend the congressman's town hall meeting in San Carlos three days later. It is this meeting that presents the photo opportunity that lands on the front page of his newsletter a few months later: Congressman Tom Lantos holds me in his arms as the face of the rare disease community for which he fights. My dad's sister, my mom's aunt, my grandmother, and other relatives all write their representatives and urge them to support the legislation. Despite some controversial elements unrelated to the Commission on Orphan Diseases, the NIH Reauthorization Bill is adopted.

As wonderful as they are, though, the NIH Reauthorization Bill (the 1983 version as well as later amendments) and ODA are not perfect. And, by 1985, calls for tax reform result in President Reagan submitting a plan to Congress that would revoke the tax credits granted to pharmaceutical companies for their involvement in the development of orphan drugs. Once again, the National Organization for Rare Disorders (NORD) urges families to write their congresspersons regarding the infinite value of the estimated $18 million cost to taxpayers. As *Times-Tribune* staff writer James Kilpatrick so eloquently states, "For the victims of rare diseases and their often desperate families, no tax loss could have greater meaning." Ultimately, that year, the "orphan drug" designation is expanded to encompass all conditions affecting fewer than 200,000 patients.

The act's continuing controversy stems from abuses by pharmaceutical companies. Because of loopholes in the legislation, certain medications obtain "orphan" status as treatments for a rare disease, but are later expanded to treat other diseases as well. The company manufacturing the drug obtains the benefits of the ODA but reaps large amounts of profit due to physicians prescribing the drug for other conditions. There are also drugs, such as those used in the treatment of AIDS, that initially have a fairly small market, but as the market expands, they hold on to their orphan drug status despite, again, reaping enormous profits. Other medications, such as human growth hormone, are developed for a very specific condition and then adopted by vanity clinics seeking to appeal to a generation of baby boomers in need of anti-aging treatments. While it remains illegal for a pharmaceutical company to market a product for an unapproved purpose, nothing prevents physicians from prescribing it.

Despite the controversies and potential abuses, the Orphan Drug Act persists, and the cystinosis community greatly benefits from the resulting incentives that ultimately lead Mylan Pharmaceuticals to develop a marketable version of cysteamine capsules (Cystagon). Still, cysteamine doesn't achieve FDA approval until a decade after I start taking it, but it does so in part because of my participation in clinical trials made possible by the Orphan Drug Act. While as a child I still haven't found a way to alleviate my tremendous thirst, turning cysteamine into a drug that somebody will make ensures that I will hold onto my native kidneys much longer than would have previously been possible, with future generations able to do the same.

ruminations from the rink

One thing is for certain: I am an incredibly unique creation! When I attended cystinosis conferences every other year in San Diego growing up, there were so few patients available for research that I was (in those early years) offered money to participate in studies by way of psychometric testing, eye exams, MRIs, visual-spatial testing, and more, all conducted on site at UCSD. (The MRI was by far the most appealing, as I made a handsome $15 profit simply by peacefully resting inside a radiation chamber.) It goes without saying, then, that finding enough test subjects for drug trials has always been a challenge in our little rare disease community. When I participated in the original cysteamine study and then the phosphocysteamine study (and finally, the ideal dosing study) in the 1980s and early 1990s, I was always part of a group of less than 120 nationwide.

Fortunately, though, now every patient diagnosed with cystinosis is immediately put on cysteamine therapy (assuming a knowledgeable doctor is involved in the diagnosis process). We are still orphans in the sense that our needs are often overlooked, but I do see myself as one of the parents of the current generation of cystinosis orphans and am thankful that by participating in research studies made possible by the Orphan Drug Act, today's children don't have to endure the same fights—even when the disease hasn't necessarily become any less rare. **Perhaps it is a stretch to say that I have parented so many orphans, but at the same time, I know that our impact on future generations can never be fully known.** When you go through your daily battles, do you ever stop to consider that you might be fighting so others don't have to later on? Through your struggles, you are a blessing and an example—even if you don't realize it.

Rolling forward...

seven | celebrating the birthday I would never live to see

It's nice to be here. When you're 99 years old, it's nice to be anyplace.

George Burns

'Tis very certain the desire of life prolongs it.

Lord Byron

The arrival of cystinosis into our lives in 1983 creates an initial earthquake and subsequent aftershocks as my parents first come to terms with my diagnosis and then try to manage my illness and maintain normal lives for themselves and both of their daughters. In 1984, my mom works in the local school district teaching English as a Second Language. She daily encounters nine- and ten-year-old children and realizes that her own child is not expected to live beyond that point. The emotional stress of living with this reality leads her to jot down a heavy journal entry.

> *I think it is very fortunate that we can't see the future. If you knew you'd die at a certain age, everything would be planned with that in mind. Do you know we raise our kids with the future in mind? We often ask, "What are you going to be when you grow up?" So what if you are told that your child won't grow up? A psychiatrist was giving me some tips and he said he knew a family whose eight-year-old son was dying of cancer. The family was miserable, the child was doing poorly in school, etc. Come to find out, they were treating him like a child without a future—so different from others. He had no incentive, no hope, etc. When they realized this and changed their behavior and outlook, family life became more pleasant.*

After the initial diagnosis, Jessica had a second test to confirm it.

Maybe, I thought, it is all a mistake.

Those results came back and I hit another low point.

After a few weeks, I began to ask the doctor to put me in touch with other parents. He couldn't because he didn't know of any.

The Cystinosis Foundation was a complete Godsend.

The joy has come back to our household. We enjoy everything.

But just sometimes in the middle of the night I wake up crying for my child who doesn't have a future.

It is on this backdrop that I grow up, excited for each new day. Although I am completely unaware of those dark moments in 1984 and by the time I enter elementary school my parents no longer worry themselves endlessly with whether or not I will live to see another day, my family still knows that turning ten will be a milestone for me. I have much less ambitious goals, however. When I am five, I tell my friend that I cannot wait to turn seven.

"Why?" she asks.

"Because then I will be almost grown up!" I tell her.

But age seven comes and goes, I am still ordering Happy Meals at McDonald's and unable to stay home by myself, and I start thinking of future birthdays.

For I never doubt that I will turn ten, or that I will get a driver's license as a teenager, or that I will start college at age eighteen, or that I will someday get married. I may not ever put it into words, but there is always the underlying assumption that life will continue. For my parents, though—once told that I would die before my second decade of life—my tenth birthday approaches with great expectancy. Mind you, that anticipation is not for my death; it is for the chance to celebrate life with great fanfare.

So in the summer of 1991, an invitation goes out to the many prayer warriors who petitioned God on my behalf from the time of my diagnosis.

When Jessica was diagnosed with nephropathic cystinosis
at age twenty-two months, all the information indicated that
children with this rare disease usually die by age ten.
Through the grace of God, we found an effective research program
and got Jessica into it. The experimental drug Jessica is on
has slowed down the progression of this disease.

We want to praise the Lord on July 14, 1991,
the day Jessica Britt will be ten!

Please join Ernest and Gayle Britt in
thanking and praising God on
July 14, 1991
From 2:00 to 4:00
at
The Fireside Room
Peninsula Covenant Church

My tenth birthday has more significance for my parents than it does for me. Don't get me wrong; I enjoy the party. There is one gift in particular that I positively adore: a hand-sewn baseball vest made with love by my mom's best friend. I wear that vest for the rest of the party and later don it for my first (and only) baseball game at Candlestick Park. (Who the Giants play that day is unimportant, but I am tremendously well dressed and stylish for the occasion.)

At the celebration of my milestone birthday, God's position in an equation that the doctors had provided us with is made clear: I am alive because God wants it to be so. So even more than celebrating my ten years of life, the party is designed to highlight God's provision for all of us.

We sing hymns that day. Not the newer songs that I am by now used to at our contemporary church service, but the old, timeless hymns that I remember from my very young days at the Church of Christ on Madison Avenue and that I still sing when we visit my grandparents in Pecos, Texas. These are the songs that I remember hearing before reading, as I sat scribbling on a bulletin or playing in someone's lap. These are the songs that remind me of my grandfather's voice, singing the bass clef parts as I am silent. These are the words that will remain with me forever.

> *There is a God (There is a God)*
> *He is alive (He is alive)*
> *In Him we live (In Him we live)*
> *And we survive (And we survive)*

In addition to *Our God, He Is Alive,* the songs we sing are many: *Bless His Holy Name, Thy Loving Kindness, Sing and Be Happy, El Shaddai, In His Time, How Great Thou Art, To God Be The Glory,* and the *Doxology.* After my dad's welcome and a family friend's opening prayer, my mom stands in front of our friends and family and thanks God for the small things over the years, such as getting a nearby parking place at the hospital so we won't be frazzled when we arrive in the doctor's office. She praises God for my ability to tolerate my medication and for the lessons she has learned since I first became sick.

Our scripture theme that day is Psalm 92:1-2 (NKJV): *It is good to give thanks to the Lord, and to sing praises to Your name, O Most High; To declare Your lovingkindness in the morning, and Your faithfulness every night.* The overwhelming feeling behind all the sentiments expressed is that God is owed thanks.

Despite my parents' request for no gifts, I am showered with flowers, balloons, and cards. (Ironically, I later doodle on the back of one of the cards a picture of the large capsules I have just started swallowing whole.) As I play with my friends and enjoy the cake and attention that day, I am grateful that my doctors—and my God—have given my parents an excuse to throw a party. And that is about the only thought I have regarding the miracle of turning ten. I am already looking forward to the day I will turn thirteen and will finally be able to call myself a teenager, like my sister.

I am a child with a future, and that future looks bright.

ruminations from the rink

At times I think that those living with terminal illness have the brightest futures of all. Grateful for each new day to see the sun rise yet again, a person who has a chronic condition will be led to always appreciate tomorrow. Of course, one may argue that the most important thing is to appreciate today, and we do that, too. But when it is unclear how many tomorrows we will have, each one is precious. They all represent opportunities to grab the bull by the horns and prove everyone wrong.

I have proven doctors wrong. I have proven geneticists wrong. I have proven those within the rare disease community wrong. But all of this pales in comparison to proving my own mother wrong. I have lived to love her far more days than she thought I had. It is the least I can do for the woman who sacrificed so much for me.

It is not for me to imagine what it is like to have a child diagnosed with a rare, fatal illness. I cannot possibly understand the gratitude that comes with being able to throw a tenth birthday party for someone who wasn't supposed to be there to celebrate it. But I have seen small glimpses of what it is like to expect tragedy and be given victory. It is very humbling to know that I have provided my parents with a victory story. I reached ten. I reached twenty. I reached thirty. What will I do with each new day to celebrate? It is because of them that I truly live, all the days of my life.

In the famous ancient Sumerian myth, *The Epic of Gilgamesh,* King Gilgamesh learns that he cannot live forever. No one can. (Except for the Immortal One, who happens to be the Sumerian equivalent of Noah.) So we need to live for what we have and do our best to leave something behind as a legacy through which we can continue to live. I hope that whenever my time comes to meet the God in whom I have lived and survived, the words I pen in this book will be left behind as my legacy of thankfulness and joy.

What do you hope your legacy will be?

Rolling forward...

eight | two equals one

I am twelve. I am just gaining a cognizance of my own academic ability, particularly in math. It is a sad coincidence that I am at that awkward age where academic achievement is not necessarily something I want to be known for; this doesn't impact the pride I feel when a teacher puts my work on the wall, but it does mean that I am sometimes prone to laziness and a lack of effort or pursuit of excellence. As I finish my seventh grade year, my math teacher expresses her interest in recommending me for the highest class offered at the school at the time, Algebra I.

In this tracked environment of the early 1990s, few schools have started pushing their students into Algebra I, Geometry, and beyond in the eighth grade. My school has four levels in math: remedial instruction, standards-based eighth grade math, accelerated eighth grade math, and Algebra I. I shy away from being placed on an academic pedestal and instead tell my teacher and parents that I'd like to go into the accelerated class.

That summer, we attend a cystinosis family conference at UCSD. I am entering the transitional social phase where I feel too "old" to associate with the young children in conference child care, but the medical jargon of the main session also doesn't hold my attention. I spend time in the children's room but as soon as I am able, I make my way to find my parents after one of the presentations.

I am puzzled by what I encounter. It would seem that the most recent speaker addressed the area of academic difficulties in children with cystinosis. Although I'm sure this isn't what was said, I hear that all children with cystinosis struggle with math. (In fact, it was certainly stated that there are exceptions to this rule.)

Even in my mom's notebook, there is a hastily written note: *she may never become an engineer or do well in geometry.*

Some parents eagerly chat about the presentation while I wait for my parents to gather their conference materials.

"This explains SO much," one mother says. "My child absolutely cannot do math. Now I understand that it isn't his fault, and that we've been placing too much pressure on him."

"Oh, I know," says another. "Cystinotic children are so auditory. Mine is having a hard time with the visual elements of math, too. She doesn't line up the numbers properly when adding."

"This is only going to get harder as they grow up." The first mother is shaking her head. "I'll need to meet with my son's teachers and explain why he can't do the regular curriculum."

I ponder what I've overheard. Isn't math my best subject? I may not be going into the top math class at my school in the eighth grade, but wasn't I given the option? Am I a fraud?

In fact, I go through the rest of my junior high and high school career feeling like I'm somehow "faking" my mathematical talents. In ninth grade, my Honors Algebra teacher tells me that I don't belong in his class, and that to challenge myself I should take Honors Geometry concurrently so that I can enter Honors Trigonometry by my sophomore year. He also enlists my help as a classroom aid for his remedial math class. All the while, I feel like there has been some horrible mistake—I am getting answers correct on my homework and on tests, but surely it is a fluke. I don't really understand what I'm doing. Do I?

By the time I enter Honors Pre-Calculus, I am known as one of the top students in my class. In the next year's Advanced Placement Calculus class, I compete with another student, a friend who also happens to be in the school's orchestra with me. The day after every chapter test and every exam, he and I eagerly run to the grade sheet, organized by student number. I know his number and he knows mine, so with every posted test result, one of us groans at a careless mistake that inevitably led the other to take the coveted top position.

For a long time, though, I can't get it out of my head that I am not supposed to be able to do this task. At every turn, I question my abilities—am I somehow cheating? Do all the other students understand the material better than I do, while I simply calculate answers to difficult calculus problems without the conceptual foundation to know what the numbers, symbols, and variables mean? In school, I am obsessed with math, but I can't help feeling that I am hiding some terrible secret from my teachers, parents, and classmates: I can't really do it. I sheepishly receive a math award every year of high school at the geeky math awards night, finally culminating my senior year with a top honor in calculus. I am sure that I am unworthy.

It is only the report card grade that boosts my confidence. It is not my own perceived talent for math. At the end of my high school career, I guiltily accept a scholarship from the Society of Women Engineers to attend the University of California, Berkeley, where I have been accepted as an Electrical Engineering and Computer Science (EECS) major.

It isn't until many years later that I finally embrace my ability. As I am explaining to one of my students—an eighth grader so much more mathematically brilliant than I could ever hope to be—the concept of a derivative, it sinks in: I know this. I understand this. And I love this. It is not what I am most passionate about, as I discover in college as an EECS major who later switches to cultural studies, but it is a great love of mine nonetheless.

I miss math. I teach group sessions of algebra twice a week when school is in session and do private tutoring in algebra and geometry throughout the year, but it still sometimes feels as though my days are lacking in numerical and abstract analysis. There are few academic subjects, aside from history, that bring me so much pleasure.

Sometimes when the students in my history classes get off topic, I give them the most severe reprimand I can think of.

"You're going on the Fourth Crusade right now," I warn. "Let's set our minds to the task at hand."

In the Fourth Crusade, the Western Christians intended to wrestle Jerusalem away from the Muslims. Along the way, though, they got sidetracked and invaded and sacked the Christian city of Constantinople, killing a great many coreligionists. *Oops.*

For all my harsh admonishments, however, I occasionally go on my own Fourth Crusade. I let it slip one afternoon while with my eighth graders that there is a way to prove that two equals one. My assertion is met with looks of disbelief.

"Really," I say. "I'll show you." I proceed to offer up a relatively simple proof that is certainly not one of my own invention, but one that is as old, perhaps, as modern math textbooks. It is a proof that my calculus teacher first shared with me:

Define variables	Let $x = y$
Multiply both sides by x	$x^2 = xy$
Subtract y^2 from both sides	$x^2 - y^2 = xy - y^2$
Factor using the Difference of Squares algebraic principle on the left and simple factoring on the right	$(x + y)(x - y) = y(x - y)$
Divide both sides by x - y	$x + y = y$
Since we initially let x = y, we can use substitution to rewrite	$y + y = y$
Collect like terms	$2y = y$
Dividing both sides by y	$2 = 1$

Jaws drop. My eighth graders are distressed.

"How can that be? You're right—you proved it!" My history buff is duly impressed, as are most of his classmates.

There is one boy, though, who is frowning. "This can't be right. You must have done something wrong."

"I did," I tell him. "I did something that is not allowed." I let him search the whiteboard for my mistake. If there is anything I have learned in my years of teaching, it is that students love nothing more than to prove their instructors wrong. And I enjoy letting them, for the day a student believes that I am always right is the day that I have lost my ability to be an effective teacher.

When he finally gives up, I tell him to pay attention to the step in which I divided both sides by $x - y$. "But if we initially let $x = y$, then what are we really placing in the denominator in that step?"

"Zero! You divided by zero! That's illegal in algebra, and it renders your whole proof incorrect."

"True," I tell him. "But what if it weren't illegal? What if we could somehow define a new branch of mathematics in which it is perfectly okay to divide by zero? Then my proof would be correct and in that new branch of mathematics, two would equal one." In considering alternative rules, I am thinking of non-Euclidian geometry, a curious branch of mathematics that defies the parallel postulate of Euclidean geometry by asserting that planes exist on curved surfaces rather than flat ones. For example, in Euclidean geometry, the interior angles of a triangle always add up to 180 degrees. In non-Euclidean geometry, the interior angles of a triangle would not necessarily have 180 degrees if that triangle existed on a spherical plane.

He offers an emphatic response. "You can't do that. Once you say that the impossible is possible, then anything is possible! Even the nonsensical!"

"But what *if*," I persist. "What *if* you were allowed to do that one impossible step?"

He shrugs. "It would never end. You would be able to do anything."

"Yes," I say. "Never forget it, Sean. Once you allow yourself to do the impossible, the possibilities are limitless."

"Are we talking about math? Or are we talking about life?"

I am pleased that my top student has finally caught on. "Life." I continue, "If you learn nothing else from me this year, at least learn this: live your life without limits. Don't ever let anyone tell you that something is impossible. You never know when dividing by zero will make all the difference in the world."

I drive home that day with wet cheeks. I have found my purpose. And of course, it was math that led me there.

ruminations from the rink

Math represents to me a little microcosm of the universe; we are all faced with conundrums that require time and effort to solve, and we all delight in finding the right answers to these problems.

But math also includes rules and restrictions that are, at times, analogous to life. Just as division by zero is impossible, so too is roller skating with rickets. Or living with cystinosis past the age of ten. Or achieving the top calculus grade in your class after being told that you won't be successful in the subject. Or entering a prestigious university's engineering department despite a note, scribbled by your parent on a piece of paper many years ago after consultation with a top researcher, claiming that you will probably never become an engineer.

The impossible is possible. You just have to bend (or break) a few rules and trust that God will take care of the details and hold you firmly (and tenderly) in His hands. For the word *impossible* is not in God's vocabulary.

Rolling forward…

nine | gravity pulls up

Three words were in the captain's heart.
He shaped them soundlessly with his trembling lips,
as he had not breath to spare for a whisper, "I am lost."
And having given up life, the captain suddenly began to live.
Carson McCullers

Better to strengthen your back than lighten your burden.
Anonymous

As I prepare to start my junior year of high school, I don't think about my imminent kidney failure; or at least, I don't allow such thoughts to linger. I still experience a lot of residual guilt, left over from my period of noncompliance. Furthermore, each blood test feels analogous to taking an exam for which I haven't studied. Every one-tenth increase in my creatinine seems to be my own fault. I feel entirely out of control and wholly guilty all at the same time. These conflicting emotions lead me to focus on something I do have power over: my own academic success. I sign up for a demanding set of classes and ready myself for a deluge of scholastic rigor.

But in the weeks before school starts, it is determined that I must decide on a dialysis modality and have my blood drawn every two weeks. My levels are steadily worsening, and I experience an immense feeling of dread every time my mom checks her e-mail the morning after I've been to the lab—for even before everyone else starts doing it years later, she receives my results electronically from one of the renal nurse practitioners.

Compounding my shame is the knowledge that my quickly rising phosphorus level is within my control; my milk consumption is to blame. But when you've relied on a gallon of milk a day for sustenance for the majority of your life and for all of your mindful existence, it isn't easy to follow the doctor's orders to "eat less dairy." I feel certain that everyone is mad at me for not obeying; it does not occur to me that this is what tough love looks like and that it is breaking my parents' hearts as well.

Then there's the economic problem. Being in the military system has been fantastic until this point; the Army, Navy, and Air Force hospitals that I've gone to for my care don't even *have* billing departments. But Stanford Hospital has a very aggressive one, and we are told that if I do not upgrade my military coverage, any hospitalizations I experience at Stanford prior to my third dialysis treatment (when Medicare kicks in) will be billed directly to us. My parents scramble to enroll me in Champus Prime insurance.

I seem to be nothing but trouble.

It comes as no surprise, then, when we receive an urgent message from the renal nurse practitioner. My mom prints the e-mail and sets in on the dining room table; it screams back at me with a threatening gravity that forces my attention downward: *PLEASE CALL ME AT THE OFFICE TODAY! Jessica's creatinine is 7.3 and her phosphorus a whopping 9.9! How is she feeling? Does she have shortness of breath? Trouble concentrating? Swelling?*

The only thing I'm having trouble concentrating on is what this all means. I do not allow it to become my reality, even when my previously scheduled November 14 appointment is moved up by a week. I am shuffled from nurse practitioner to doctor and finally to the surgeon, who tells me that I will be having my dialysis permacatheter placed on November 11, a rare mid-week Veterans' Day holiday at school. My mom questions the necessity of the surgery so soon and tells them all that I don't seem to feel so bad. The truth is, I have stopped allowing myself to feel at all. I just am; outside of my school life, I merely exist.

The day before my surgery, fear remains lodged somewhere in the depths of my mind as I move from class to class. Advanced Physics is quickly becoming one of my least favorite subjects this year; although I end up earning an award for being one of my school's top physics students, the teacher is new and significantly lacking in classroom management skills. I learn very little in the way of science.

Our classroom desks are designed for four students, with a computer on each table for motion experiments. In the late 1990s, computer mice aren't infrared—they have track balls inside of them. In a classroom where I learn more about my teacher's love life (he is dating a ballerina who is, apparently, quite agile) than I do about Newton's Second Law of Motion, my table mates and I often find ourselves taking out the mice orbs and playing silly tabletop games.

There is a senior at my table, Shane. He and I are "physics friends" only, and we never associate outside of class. We are prone to getting in trouble for playing with the computer accessories, and on November 10 after a particularly successful game of mouse ball catch, we are told to stay after class and clean all the tables, computer keyboards, and mice.

Shane and I clean the tables slowly. It is as if neither of us is in a hurry for what awaits us in the lunchroom. We are silent for a while, clearly resenting our duties but also somewhat enjoying the peace and quiet, which are so rare for this classroom.

I have a lot on my mind. I have no idea what tomorrow really means. I have no recollection of the sedation I underwent at time of diagnosis, and I haven't been under general anesthesia since. Now, I am about to have a tube surgically placed in my chest. If anyone at school is aware of my situation, it certainly isn't because I have uttered a word. I pride myself in knowing that no one would guess that I have a genetic condition that is slowly destroying my cells.

At some point, though, all that bottled-up-inside fear gets to me. "I'm having surgery tomorrow," I blurt.

Shane doesn't miss a beat. "What are you having done?"

"My kidneys don't work. I'm going to have to be hooked up to a huge mechanical kidney three times a week. The surgery is to put a tube in so my blood can be taken out, filtered, and put back in."

He stops and looks up from the mouse he is polishing with a damp tissue. "Woah. That sounds kind of big."

"Yeah."

"So your friends know?"

"Not at all. My friends don't even know that I have a disease that caused the kidney failure in the first place."

He frowns slightly. "So why are you telling me?"

"Because you're not my friend." I am talking quickly now. "I don't have to worry about you treating me differently within the context of friendship, because we don't have one."

"Gee, thanks. But you really don't think your friends would understand?"

"I think they would treat me differently. Not necessarily badly, but in a way that I wouldn't want to be treated. Like they feel sorry for me or something. Like I have some sort of burden that I have to carry."

"But you do... right?"

"No. It's not a burden. It's just life."

"Don't you think your friends would be impressed with your strength?"

He doesn't get it. I don't want to be admired, either, because that points to some strange belief that cystinosis should impact me so much that I can't do the things I do—or that it is impressive that I do them in spite of some hardship. "Yes."

"So what's the problem? You don't want people to pity you for what you go through, but you don't want them to be impressed, either."

I think about this. At the moment, I do seem to be impossibly annoying. What do I want? "Sometimes you want to be known for who you are, and not for what you have or what you do."

"Jess, you're already known for certain things, at least as I understand it. You're known for being good at math, for one thing. That's something that you do."

"But I'm good at it in spite of nothing. Not in spite of kidney failure, or a disease, or some other hardship. It shouldn't be impressive owing to the fact that I have a genetic disease. It just is. It's a part of who I am. Cystinosis really isn't." Although my mind will later change on this final point, I state it unequivocally.

"Well, if you ever want to talk to a non-friend about it, let me know. I'm here."

"Thanks."

At the end of our punishment, our teacher thanks us and announces his decision that Shane and I can't handle sitting at the same table. The two of us never have another conversation.

My surgery is thankfully eventful only in its unfamiliarity to me. As I am wheeled into the operating room shortly before noon, any semblance of nervousness is easily suppressed by the mild sedatives I am receiving through my IV. I enjoy the feeling of weightlessness and lightened anxiety that pulses through my body.

The room is bright, with startling white walls and vivid blue scrubs surrounding me on all sides. I blink quickly but do not squint. I want to remember this. I want to take in everything I can and learn precisely what is being done. Before I am able to start questioning my caregivers, though, my vision is filled with the face of a kind-looking man with greying temples. He tells me that he is going to help me go to sleep.

I have always trusted men with greying temples. It occurs to me that they have nothing to hide, as they have not bothered to conceal their advancing years and growing wisdom. Yet they are not quite grey enough to make careless mistakes owing to old age. When I think about the Sundays of my more carefree youth, I remember sitting on my father's lap in a pew at First Christian Church on Topaz Street and noticing, above all else, the patches on the elbows of his suit coat and the greying temples that framed his handsome face. I particularly like airplane pilots with greying temples.

Greying Temples tells me to count backwards from ten. Being the sassy teenager that I am, I ask him if I go into negative numbers once I reach zero. He tells me that will be unnecessary.

"But I am fully awake," I say. I'm pretty sure my speech is slurring.

"All right," Greying Temples appeases me with a knowing smile. "If you reach zero, you may go negative."

10...9...8...7... I pause. What number am I on? Oh yes, 8. I plan to prove this silly anesthesiologist wrong; *8...7...6...*

I often wonder what my surgical dreams are like and what fantastical lands I visit while in this state of bliss.

Just after 1:30 that afternoon, I awake to a stiffness below my right collarbone. It doesn't hurt as long as I don't move. The permacath placement choice is due in part to my passion for playing the violin; the surgeon had told us that a fistula would disfigure my arm and possibly interfere with my musical pursuits. But as I am still and alone on the gurney awaiting the arrival of family, I still feel disfigured. Without looking down, I know that there are now tubes uncouthly hanging out of my body. My days of wearing fashionable low-neck tops (which, admittedly, never really began) are over. The days of my native kidneys doing their job are also over; a large, unnatural one requiring a wall outlet and filters and tubes will take their place. I feel cyborg, half human, and most importantly, not normal—for the first time in my life.

ruminations from the rink

Newton's First Law is famous for its paraphrase: an object in motion tends to stay in motion; an object at rest tends to stay at rest.

Starting with my noncompliance, I led a life in which my health consistently spiraled downward and out of my control. Although where this spiral led wasn't necessarily my fault, I couldn't emotionally face the hopelessness of losing my kidneys and depending on a machine for life, so I turned my back on feelings related to my health entirely. In hindsight, I see that this was an immensely difficult period; at the time, though, my primary concerns were academic achievement and social competence.

Though I didn't know it, the weightiness of my condition required relief. The downward gravitational pull of reality—the need for dialysis catheter placement surgery—propelled my life into a trajectory that was eventually acted upon by an outside force and edited. Ironically, this force came in the classroom where Newton's laws were studied. By telling a fellow physics student about my rapidly declining health, a burden was lifted. **Although I never told any of my school friends about dialysis, sharing with a relative stranger allowed me to experience a previously unknown lightness just prior to a very heavy surgery.**

I never had to go through any of my medical challenges alone; I always had immense support from my family and my church. But I desperately needed another listening ear, and I found a willing one. I didn't need the stronger back that was bound to develop anyway; a lighter burden, though, was an unexpected gift.

What are you going through that might be pulling you down? It is likely that those around you want to help. Let them—the result will be immensely uplifting.

Rolling forward…

ten | dependency yields independence

Later on the afternoon of my catheter placement surgery, I receive my first dialysis treatment in my hospital room. It is completely unreal. I am still under the influence of various pain medications and residual anesthetics. I hear my mom ask the doctor if dialysis is really necessary, given that my creatinine has gone down to 5.3. He tells her it is time.

Most people with end-stage renal failure who are on dialysis have to have a certain amount of fluid removed in the process, since their kidneys are not producing enough urine. Fortunately for someone with cystinosis, Fanconi syndrome (which is not corrected until transplant, or when the native kidneys fully shut down) persists, and my excessive thirst—and excessive urination—remain intact. My first dialysis treatment is two hours short, and it goes in my record as a standing order for future dialysis nurses that I am not to have fluid removed.

I am visited by a young couple from our church, Charlie and Nancy, who work with high school students. My soon to be brother-in-law brings me flowers, which are later removed from my room because the floor I'm staying on has bone marrow transplant patients. My mom spends the night in the hospital room with me and makes sure that I get doses of Cystagon at 9:00 p.m. and 3:00 a.m. It comes as a relief to learn that I will be receiving epoetin through the dialysis machine from now on; no more at-home shots necessary to treat my anemia. Polycitra and Rocaltrol will also be given through the machine. Apparently, this dialysis thing has its perks. In a world where I have numbed myself to what it all really means for my life and my long-term future, hearing that next Thursday's injection is not necessary is a monumental relief.

It is unknown at this point whether I will need dialysis a full three times a week or if I will get by with less for a long period. I'm started on a twice-a-week schedule. The polycitra decision is reversed—apparently I'm not a typical dialysis patient, and my Fanconi syndrome requires daily treatment. I'll continue to drink 15 cc of the vile green liquid four times per day.

My first dialysis session as an outpatient takes place late one evening at the Stanford adult dialysis unit rather than the cozy pediatric room, which holds more reasonable hours. I am immediately struck by the assembly line nature of the room. I am hooked up to the machine while uninterested patients on either side of me stare blankly ahead. A man at the far end of the room is snoring softly. There are no family members in this room, no visitors, no cheerful wallpaper or patient photos adorning the walls. My face indicates no emotion, though I whimper softly as my bandages are changed. The heart sinkage I experience upon hearing that my bandages will need to be changed at every session is indescribable. I don't think about how long this will last, but I know that this moment, this evening, this room—it's all dreary. I can't wait for the next day's math class. I enjoy the satisfaction of solving difficult proofs using trigonometric functions.

At this point I don't know what an uneventful dialysis session is like, because everything is new. The nurse hooking me up to the machine certainly acts as though everything is routine for her, even if it isn't for me. I watch my blood as it gradually turns the clear tube running out of my body red. I watch as the filter in the machine slowly soaks up the crimson. The color spreads, like a pestilence, until it moves back into my body via the other, once transparent tube, now also opaque with my blood. I imagine the lines as a cyborg artery and vein. I watch the clock.

I near the halfway point of my dialysis treatment—only scheduled for two hours today—when all of a sudden, everything is wrong. I am overtaken by severe chills. I feel hot and cold at the same time. My shaking makes my dialysis catheter jump and shift and my new electronic kidney blares its siren. The nurse rushes to my side to see what is going on. In the three or four seconds it takes for all of this to happen, I feel certain that my life is coming to an end.

The nurse isn't talking to me. I'm groaning and desperately trying to stop my own shaking. Now there's a thermometer in my ear. The machine is silenced. I plead with her not to uncover me to remove the tubing, because I feel cold as ice. She tells me that she has no choice; I have to be unhooked and my lines flushed to prevent clotting. She also assures me that I am not cold. I have a fever of 103.9. Some assurance.

There is now a steady stream of tears falling down my face. The shaking is completely exhausting and thoroughly painful, because it is forcing excessive movement in my upper body, where I am still sore from surgery.

"C-c-c-an I p-p-p-lease have another h-h-heated bl-bl-blanket?" I am so cold.

"Let me page the doctor on call first. It's late and your nephrologist has gone home. You might need to be admitted to the hospital."

"Wait… admitted?" The shaking has not subsided, but suddenly I am speaking quite clearly. "I have school tomorrow."

She ignores me and puts the phone receiver down without taking her eyes off it. It rings almost immediately. She must have paged the doctor a special code to let him know that she is dealing with a medical emergency. That doesn't do much to expunge my fears that I'm going to go into a coma—or worse. She explains my situation. Then she is silent for a very long time as she takes in his response.

I am trying to will my quivering body to be still. I hold my breath. I grip the armrests on my dialysis chair. I exhale deeply. I try all methods of calming myself down and warming up, including picturing myself on a tropical island. I think the people who suggest such fantasies must have very active imaginations. Unfortunately, I remain firmly grounded in my own reality. I am not on a warm beach. I am in a dialysis chair, experiencing what feels like subzero temperatures inside my body while my skin feels hot as the hair straightening iron that once burned the back of my ear.

When the doctor enters, I am briefly distracted from my pain. He is wearing the recognizable white coat and stethoscope typical of a physician, but cowboy boots peak out of his dark pants. He seems calm but competent, ready to take charge and problem solve. Most of all, in my sea of shivering, he looks like the warm island that my mind had been unable to conjure.

"Demerol," he says to the nurse, handing her a vial of medication. She begins prepping a syringe to put the clear liquid in my line. The warm cowboy turns to me. "Dr. Alex," he says, holding out his hand.

I shake it. "Hi," I say through my chattering teeth.

He rolls over one of the chairs and sits at my side while the nurse injects the Demerol. "That should stop the chills and make you a little sleepy in a few minutes." This is a new experience for me. A doctor has pulled up a chair and is sitting with me, talking to me face-to-face, without my parents. "Let's talk about what's going on."

After I describe how I'm feeling, he lays out my options. "We could send you home as planned, and you can return for dialysis on Thursday. The problem is, my guess is that you have an infection in your line and this will happen every time we try to dialyze you." I want so badly to go home, but his reasoning sounds fair. "We could send you home with a catch-all antibiotic and hope that it clears up the problem. Or we could admit you and diagnose what exactly is going on and treat you and give you in-patient dialysis to make sure we've taken care of the issue."

I sigh. The shaking has finally stopped. From the moment the nurse had mentioned the possibility of admitting me, I had prepared myself to fight against it until the only way to get me into yet another hospital gurney was to overcome my forceful kicking and screaming.

I grow up a lot in the minute I take to contemplate Dr. Alex's words. I'm in the adult dialysis unit without my parents. A physician is talking to me as if I am in control of my own destiny tonight. He is not standing over me, telling me what will happen to me next. He has literally put himself at my level and is looking me in the eye. He seems to respect my thoughts and trust my ability to take the facts and make an informed decision.

"I guess I need to be admitted," I say.

Dr. Alex smiles and pats my knee, silently assuring me that I have made the right decision. I don't know. Maybe it never was my decision and he always planned on admitting me, regardless of my answer. But I feel older, more responsible, and more involved with my own health. He rolls his chair over to the phone. I close my eyes, suddenly comforted by the return of my own body heat. I am sleepy.

"Jessica." My eyelids open halfway. Dr. Alex is looking up from the paperwork he is filling out by the phone. "I need your phone number so that I can talk to your mom or dad."

I frown, or at least, I think I turn the corners of my mouth downwards and furrow my brow a bit. I am so sleepy and my muscles are so relaxed. I start giggling.

"What's so funny?"

"Dr. Alex, the next time you need information from me," I slur, "please ask for it before the Demerol!" For some reason, I find his order of operations—a mathematical term that immediately comes to mind— beyond hysterical.

ruminations from the rink

It became apparent in the next few days that I had septicemia, or blood poisoning through a pathogenic bacteria in my blood. It was probably contracted during my dialysis catheter placement surgery. I was put on IV antibiotics in the hospital and eventually resumed dialysis without incident.

Within a couple weeks, I requested a permanent physician change to Dr. Alex. He changed my entire existence. I have no doubt that I was headed to a bad place. Though I can't say I ever looked forward to dialysis itself, I certainly cherished the opportunity to see Dr. Alex.

I don't believe in chance or coincidence. While I do accept cause and effect and a natural sequence of events, I also believe all things to be part of God's divine providence.

I heard a friend once say that shortly after her son started taking violin lessons, he announced to her that God had made the violin just for him. No doubt there are many thousands of little boys and girls for whom the violin exists. But for each one, God allowed it just for that individual.

Likewise, I'm sure Dr. Alex has influenced countless lives. But when God brought him from Texas to Stanford, He whispered inaudibly, "I'm putting you here just for Lenny Martinez. I'm putting you here just for Mary Thomas. *I'm putting you here just for Jessica Britt.*"

It took a couple weeks for the bacteria to be completely flushed out of my system. It was a scary and traumatic time. Looking back, though, I would gladly do it all over again. I cannot imagine what would have been had my surgery not been conducted in a problematic, less-than-sterile environment. For out of that terrible experience came a meeting with one of the people who would change my life and someone who I would later thank God for most profusely: more than any machine or medical treatment available, Dr. Alex kept me alive.

Most importantly, as I became dependent on a machine, Dr. Alex ushered me into a new era of independence and empowerment when he rolled his chair over to my dialysis station and looked me in the eye.

Rolling forward…

eleven | call the doctor! she's never been more alive

Just because I loves you
That's de reason why
Ma heart's a fluttering aspen leaf
When you pass by.

Langston Hughes

We are most alive when we're in love.

John Updike

My dialysis life isn't depressing, because I don't allow myself to think about it. Eventually, I am on so many medications both on and off the machine that I could probably open my own pharmacy. And I certainly wouldn't mind getting rid of some of this stuff on the black market. In addition to the cysteamine (in the form of Cystagon), polycitra, and Rocaltrol that I have been on for years, I am on extra iron and a weekly epoetin shot (formerly given at home by my mother, now given through the dialysis machine), two different kinds of blood pressure medicine (including a skin patch), additional bicarbonate to combat my continuing acidosis, and carnitine for muscle wasting.

When doctors broach the subject of putting me on experimental hourly eye drops, first in 1990 when I am around nine years old and now again in my teenage years, I stubbornly balk that I don't even *need* to wear sunglasses. (This is not entirely true, but the fact that I generally *refuse* to wear them, especially at cystinosis conferences where everyone else does, is a fair statement.) With so many medications and trips to the hospital, it is hardly astonishing that I am unwilling to add a new treatment requiring my attention every waking hour. And with all my other levels all over the place, a little eye discomfort is the least of my concerns, despite warnings of blindness.

Most distressing of all, because of my alarmingly high phosphorus level, I am forced to give up milk. (Dairy products are a prime source of phosphorus, and people in renal failure can have a difficult time eliminating excess phosphorus, which can then lead to brittle bones.)

Had I been living on my own and had my own source of income, I would have ignored the doctor's orders and kept drinking it. But I am sixteen. My dad simply stops buying milk from the store. I am prescribed a vile soy-based, calorie-rich drink instead; it tastes a little like Ensure. I am also told to chew five TUMS tablets every time I eat a meal or snack. The calcium can help bind with the phosphorus and remove it from the system.

Have you ever tried to eat that much flavored chalk? I lose my small appetite very quickly.

But the nature of Cystagon is that it does not react kindly to an empty stomach. Each time I take my Cystagon with water, I throw it up a half hour later. I am now told that I am not getting enough calories, so my doctor allows two cups of milk daily back into my diet. I silently wonder if perhaps throwing up a little more will earn me back the other fourteen cups I am accustomed to. Instead, though, the hospital's dietitian gives me microlipids to put in my milk to increase the number of calories. The vomiting subsides a bit, but it is still not a hugely unusual occurrence for me to throw up in the morning before leaving for school.

(When I was around seven years old and in the cysteamine study at UCSD, the research team once attempted to get me to take cysteamine on an empty stomach so that highly accurate cysteamine and cystine levels could be drawn frequently in an effort to determine when the drug peaked and was ultimately eliminated from my system. Without fail for three days while in the hospital, I threw up like clockwork fifteen, thirty, and forty-five minutes after taking my cysteamine with water. It was typically at the forty-five minute mark that I was finally given the milk I so desperately . wanted with the cysteamine I had to re-take to replace what had inevitably ended up in the vomit that was rushed to the lab for analysis.)

Now, a twenty-four-hour urine collection indicates that my kidney function is at seven percent. My dialysis treatments are increased to three-and-a-half hours three times a week. Two months after my initial dialysis catheter placement surgery, though, the tube shifts and dialysis becomes impossible. I am scheduled for another surgery. It will be my second of seven dialysis catheters. During the surgery, it is discovered that my first dialysis tube, in addition to being out of place, is also completely blocked due to a blood clot.

When I return home with my new dialysis catheter on February 2, 1998, I go immediately to bed despite the fact that it is still only late afternoon. When I wake up around 10:00 p.m., I discover that I am soaked in blood. At this point, all I can do is sigh and drag myself into the living room, where my mom is doing some of her work.

"Mom?" I say, unsure quite how to break the news that there is blood pouring out of my surgical site.

Fortunately, I don't have to. She looks up from her work—and then immediately straightens in her seat, alarmed. Before I am fully aware of her reaction, she is handing me a towel and telling me to press it against the wound and we are rushing to the emergency room. I receive one stitch to close up the hole where my previous catheter had been and am once again reminded that life is an adventure.

Aside from Shane, my peers at school don't know about my condition. Out of necessity, my teachers know, but all correspondence directed to them from the nurse's office is labeled as confidential and they are generally aware of my desire for privacy.

I have a few close friends, but I always keep myself at a proverbial arm's length away emotionally. It is probably for the best. As they head to each other's houses or downtown for some Village Host Pizza after school, three times a week I am picked up and taken to the Ambulatory Care Unit (ACU) at Lucile Packard Children's Hospital at Stanford for dialysis. On Tuesdays and Thursdays, my typical non-hospital days (when my permacath is working well enough), I feel okay but tired. After dialysis on Monday, Wednesday, and Friday, I come home feeling miserable. At first, I am invited to various social activities by my friends, or even asked to merely "hang out" in the bleachers after school. After I politely decline several times, the invitations thin out. I am a school friend only.

Things are different at church. Because I am in a small-group Bible study with several high school girls, I am encouraged to share prayer requests on a weekly basis. My initial requests are typical of the academic-scholar mask I wear at school: pray that I am able to pass my trigonometry test (and by *pass* I really mean *ace*), pray that I am able to finish my English paper on time, pray that I am willing to light a Bunsen burner in chemistry class despite my fear of searing the tips of my fingers. In time, though, I see my church peers go into deeper, more heartfelt topics with ease. It seems natural to do the same.

It is so natural, in fact, that I don't remember telling these girls about dialysis or cystinosis. I know that I do, because they are soon praying for my problematic dialysis catheter to filter blood at the rate required for a good session. They pray over each of my catheter replacement surgeries. They pray for what I haven't allowed myself to talk to God about yet: a new kidney.

And then there's the young men's Bible study group. We occasionally meet up with them for social outings like trips to San Francisco's Metreon entertainment mall or Armadillo Willy's for Southern-style barbecue.

Wayne is in that group. I noticed him for the first time in fifth or sixth grade: a loud and obnoxious—but cute—boy who sat in the back of the room with his rambunctious friends. I did my best to ignore him then as I do now, when our two groups get together about once a month.

My best isn't good enough for his persistence, though. He starts sitting near to me during Sunday-morning high school group, managing at least to get a chair at my table. I think of it as nothing more than a mild annoyance—he sits on the edge, physically between my world and his, and most of his words are still directed towards his own crowd at a neighboring table. His laugh, his mannerisms, his audacity—all of these things seem diametrically opposed to my quiet, reserved demeanor.

One Wednesday evening about a year before I start dialysis, Wayne calls me. At first, I have no idea who he is when my mom hands me the phone.

"Hi Jessica, it's Wayne."

I pause. "Hi," I say slowly enough that he can probably sense the lack of recognition in my voice.

"From church."

Oh, that Wayne. "Hi," I say again, this time with more confidence. *Why is he calling me?*

He starts talking. And talking. And talking. He is telling me about the latest fantasy book he is reading, something in the *Shannara* series by Terry Brooks. I wonder what it is about me that makes him think I care.

I am polite and in general, a good listener. I don't stop him or hint that I would rather be watching an old episode of *I Love Lucy* that I have taped and have seen a hundred times than continue talking about some fantasy world that encourages teenage boys everywhere to suppose that the ideal woman wields a knife and slays evil trolls in her spare time.

Almost as abruptly as the conversation begins, he brings it to a close with an invitation.

"Hey, do you want to go to youth group with me tonight?" Oh, that's right. It's Wednesday.

"Um… no, not this time. I have homework to do." All my homework is finished.

"Okay, well, if you change your mind, it'd be nice to see you."

We say our goodbyes and I let out a sigh of relief. I don't like the idea of going to Wednesday night youth group at church. I fear the types of close bonds that are formed at such gatherings. All that talk of how to best love one another. It isn't for me.

Wayne starts calling me every Wednesday night. I start taking showers on Wednesday nights during the hour before youth group; I figure it is easier for my mom to say I am not available than for me to politely endure his endless talking and culminating invitation to go to church. He continues to sit near me on Sunday mornings, and I continue to be annoyed.

Finally, one Wednesday shortly before starting dialysis—which would later make me unavailable on midweek nights for entirely different reasons—I get out of the shower and ask my mom if anyone called.

She says no.

I am dumbstruck. Did I hear her correctly? You could set your clock to Wayne's weekly phone call, and now, nothing?

But I am more confounded by my own feelings. Could this be… heartbreak?

No, he is far too much of a stranger to me for me to be heartbroken over my perceived loss. But I realize that it *does* feel like a loss—and I am experiencing a pang of sadness.

After that, I take an increased interest in Wayne and make more effort to get to know him. Two weeks later, his calls resume, and this time I ask if I can borrow one of his fantasy books to read for myself. I do so, and surprisingly, I love it. My opinion of the genre increases a hundredfold and my feelings for Wayne grow into something that resembles warm friendship. He still annoys me at times, but I find his loud laugh and social faux pas more endearing.

I don't remember, then, when Wayne learns about dialysis. But he does. He doesn't really talk about it. At one point, my blood pressure is such cause for concern that I am required to wear a twenty-four-hour heart monitor under my clothing. Inevitably, the day that I wear it falls on one of the days that my Bible study group and Wayne's group get together for a movie and a post-film trip to Jamba Juice.

We are sitting outside, sucking down our fruit- and vitamin-packed beverages, and I am feeling immensely uncomfortable. The heart monitor is bulky, and I am wearing a thick sweatshirt as a result—but it is a warm evening. And while I could hide in the darkness of the movie theater, the bright lights illuminating the Jamba Juice patio leave me worried that someone will notice the extra bulk I am carrying.

Wayne is next to me and we are enjoying a side conversation about his writing and the worlds that he hopes one day to create for readers everywhere. As the conversation lulls, I mention to him that I am not feeling so well.

"You probably haven't noticed, but I'm wearing a heart monitor. I have to for twenty-four hours. It's a pain. Doesn't make me want to do a whole lot."

"I noticed," he says.

"Really?" Apparently I'm not hiding the paperback-sized black box as well as I think.

"Well, I knew something was up. I mean, you're not yourself today. That stinks about the heart monitor. Hey, we should go miniature golfing next time we all get together!"

I look at this boy who sits beside me, my world positively turned upside down.

He doesn't care, I think to myself, *even though he knows.* It doesn't matter how abnormal some of my circumstances are. I am a normal sixteen-year-old girl to him. How positively glorious!

A few short weeks after the heart monitor incident, Wayne and I are walking across the small bridge on our church's campus from high school Sunday School to the main sanctuary. He stops me and examines the protruding ridge on my neck, where the top of my dialysis catheter rests right beneath the skin.

"Can I touch it?" he asks.

I am horrified. "What? No! I don't even touch it myself. Grosses me out."

"Why? I think it's cool."

"Wayne, it is *not* cool to have a tube in your neck and chest. It is even worse to be able to see it, nearly popping out like this one does. It's like," I think quickly, "seeing the outline of a rat underneath your bed's sheet. You never want to go near that bed again, let alone sleep in it."

He laughs. "But you have to live in your own skin," he says.

"Yes, but I don't go around touching rats through sheets and I'm not going to touch this—or let you," I add, predicting his next retort.

He stands there, grinning. "Can I come visit you on dialysis sometime this week?"

Again, I am mildly repulsed. "Why would you want to subject yourself to that? I had an extended family relative come once, and he fainted at the sight of it."

I think I end up agreeing for the same reason that we can't help but turn our heads to look at a wreck by the side of the road: we feel distressed and intrigued at the same time, wondering if anything earth-shattering will happen before our very eyes.

That Friday, I tell the nurse, Felix, that I might have a visitor. I am not convinced Wayne will show—but it makes sense to provide warning in case he does.

I regularly dialyze with a young man, Rudy, who comes in the early afternoons; we have about an hour of overlap before he is disconnected and I still have two or two-and-a-half hours to go. During that hour of overlap, we always watch the same shows on television, because I never ask for the remote. I usually come in as *The Rosie O'Donnell* show is ending and he switches the channel to enjoy *Animaniacs* and *Pinky and the Brain.* I don't really mind, as the television doesn't provide me with much entertainment anyway and I end up asking the nurse to just turn it off when Rudy leaves. It will be decades, certainly—centuries, maybe—before I get the *Pinky and the Brain* theme song out of my head, though. I just might end up changing the lyrics to words of praise and singing that tune in heaven.

My machine has been running for about a half hour when Wayne walks in with a videotape under his arm and a smile on his face. He looks only briefly at my machine in all its blood-filtering glory and then searches the room for a chair. My five-foot-tall nurse takes in Wayne—just over six feet tall—with interest before wheeling a chair over to us.

Wayne holds up the videotape. "Can I put this in?"

I look up at Pinky, who is doing something without much forethought that will inadvertently be more successful than any of Brain's well-thought-out schemes, and I hesitate. "Well, maybe we should wait…"

"It's okay," Rudy interjects. I forget that there are no private conversations in this room. "Go ahead." He nods at Wayne. Wayne puts the movie *Romancing the Stone* in the ACU's VCR and the three of us settle in for the Disney classic.

One of the perks of being on dialysis is that you wear a blood pressure cuff the entire time you are on the machine. Typically set to run a test every thirty minutes, my machine is programmed to check my blood pressure and pulse every fifteen minutes because I have a notoriously difficult time maintaining normal levels. Although many people with end-stage renal disease need to have the fluid removed from their bodies that their kidneys can no longer deal with, my Fanconi syndrome means that I am still urinating excessively. A high pulse indicates to the dialysis nurse that I am dehydrated and might need IV fluids.

Shortly after Wayne's arrival, my arm feels the familiar squeeze of the blood pressure cuff. I know I am on edge with Wayne—who is slowing becoming the love of my life—sitting beside me. The machine blares loudly.

Another nurse, nicknamed Cherry, has just arrived to relieve Felix during his lunch break. She rushes to the machine and the look on her face says it all: something is not right.

"Jessica!" she trills, her voice full of concern. "Your pulse is 195! We need to call a doctor *right now!*"

I frantically look from her to Felix and try to tell them with my eyes: *nothing is wrong with me. It's him. He's doing this to me.* They don't seem to be getting the hint, and Felix is already taking out his watch and double-checking my pulse while Cherry makes a beeline for the phone.

"Cherry," I say, "please don't call the doctor. I'm fine." I catch her attention and make an obvious side glance at Wayne before meeting her eyes again.

A flash of understanding crosses her face. "Oh! Well… 195 is very high. Let's check it again in five minutes."

I breathe half a sigh of relief at this decision, and I let out the other half breath when my pulse is considerably lower with the subsequent test. But I ponder the curious situation: *this boy makes my heart race.*

In September 1998, after nearly a year of dialysis, my condition takes a turn for the worse and I have a serious heart-to-heart with Dr. Alex. He tells me that I am experiencing a normal decline due to being on dialysis for a while. He again warns me about my dairy consumption, even though it has necessarily decreased. He lets me know what to expect as my senior year progresses: increased tiredness, inability to concentrate, slipping grades. I feel like Dr. Alex is being unfair when he tells me that my current course load may not be manageable, and angry tears silently fall down my cheeks as I refuse to look away from my beloved nephrologist's stern eyes.

I am uncomfortable talking about my distress with my parents, and my peers at school are of course out of the question due to the self-imposed private nature of my condition. So I go to Wayne.

"I'm going to prove the doctor wrong, you know," I tell Wayne, daring him to contradict me. "This will be my best year yet."

And it is, both academically and socially. I fall in love—with calculus, with the boy who treats me normally despite knowing about where I go and what I do three times a week, and with what I coin in my journal as FALE, the Fight Against Lowered Expectations.

Wayne visits me at dialysis a couple more times before his parents decide to pack up the family and move to Virginia in order to learn the craft of sustainable farming from a seasoned agriculturist. I am, of course, heartbroken. How things have changed since first noticing the obnoxious ten-year-old in Sunday School!

When I receive my transplant, Wayne is still in Virginia. I am adamant that someone get word to his family that the Big Day has finally come. Of all the correspondence I receive during my twelve-day initial stay in the hospital and subsequent two-week sojourn due to acute rejection, I cherish the cards from Wayne the most.

August 17, 1999

Dear Jessica,

Congratulations! You waited long enough and it came soon enough. Rest easy and take it slow. I know the doctors have said it at least a hundred times, but please listen to them just this once?

So what's it like? I haven't had a chance to experience surgery yet (and don't really want to), but it sounds interesting. Too bad I couldn't be there, as you probably have a lot of down time. Though it's nice that you don't have to worry about it interrupting school. Sorry you can't make it to Berkeley until Spring, but not too sorry. If you had gone off to college, we couldn't see each other when we come visit in November.

Love,
Wayne

And his family does indeed return about three months after my transplant. But before long, I am heading to the University of California, Berkeley and Wayne's family is heading to Oregon to start their own farm using the skills they gain while in Virginia. We naturally drift apart, and on July 14, 2001—my twentieth birthday, which I spend living among strangers in Boston after taking an engineering internship at Tufts University—Wayne calls me for the last time.

The last time, that is, until almost exactly five years later, when he calls me from Hawaii on his way home from a deployment with the United States Marine Corps to the Middle East via a Naval amphibious assault ship.

ruminations from the rink

In my two years on dialysis, the hospital became my second home, despite my unwillingness to acknowledge it as such. Ironically, the place responsible for healing was also slowing breaking my heart. Every dialysis treatment left me battered and broken in ways that no doctor could diagnose. I thought by hiding my cystinosis life from friends at school, I could somehow overcome its existence and lead a normal, happy life.

The reasoning behind this isn't sound, of course. When we hide a part of ourselves from those around us, that ugly facet of our lives doesn't magically dissolve into oblivion. It was through letting someone into my brokenness that I truly became whole. When Wayne visited me that first time at dialysis, **I was in the midst of one of the most unhealthy periods of my life—dependent on a machine, levels all over the place, calorie deficient, lethargic—and yet, suddenly, I had never been more alive.**

Although over the years the pulse story has served as my go-to "most embarrassing moment" anecdote, it also reminds me of the day that God let me know loud and clear: *you are alive when you are with Wayne Jondle.*

Rolling forward…

twelve | neither absent nor present

> There is nothing unequal as the
> equal treatment of unequals.
>
> Aristotle

> Learning is natural. School is optional.
>
> North Star Self-Directed Learning tag line

I throw myself so whole-heartedly into academic pursuits that I can hardly think of anything else. Hospital appointments, dialysis machines, kidneys—all things medical take the back burner in my mind, where I have prioritized my high school classes and my new part-time job as a technician for the San Carlos School District. But my high school's attendance policy brings my education and my health to a hazardous point of intersection.

Because of Carlmont High School's traditionally high truancy rate (for reference, it is the school on which the movie *Dangerous Minds* is based), the district establishes some strict new guidelines. We are told that more than fifteen absences, excused or unexcused, in any one class will result in a failing grade in that class and no credit awarded—regardless of whether or not the missed material is made up and all homework is turned in. In the words of the letter we receive, "absences for illness, field trips, athletics, cuts, family vacations, or any other reason" will all be counted in the tally.

I am a straight-A student. Three of my classes—Advanced Chemistry, Advanced U.S. History, and Advanced Physics—even have a policy that any student who earns higher than ninety-five percent on all tests during the semester doesn't have to take the final exam. I find myself sitting out during all three finals. Also in my junior year, I consistently earn A-pluses on my report card for Pre-Calculus. I make up all work from my absences.

But the school is rigid. During my time on dialysis, near constant catheter problems result in multiple surgeries and other hospitalizations. It isn't long before my parents are receiving letters from the school, alerting them that I am in danger of failing multiple classes and will need to attend Saturday remediation (but even then, will not receive credit if I exceed the maximum number of absences).

Failing? Huh? It feels like a slap in the face of everything I hold dear. Dialysis is not my life; academic achievement is. I've managed to keep the latter independent of the former despite Dr. Alex's predictions that end-stage renal failure might hinder my concentration. So why does the school insist on making the two unavoidably linked?

My mother composes a letter to the principal, with copies sent to the school nurse, all my teachers, and the district superintendent.

May 2, 1998

Dear Principal _____:

I am the parent of Jessica Britt, a Carlmont junior. This letter is to give you some feedback on the District attendance policy.

While I am definitely in favor of an attendance policy and believe it has had positive results, I think revision is needed because its inflexible provisions do not accommodate, but rather discriminate against a student such as Jessica who has unique difficulties.

Jessica has a health problem in which her very survival depends upon a kidney dialysis machine. She goes for dialysis at Lucile Packard Children's Hospital at Stanford three days a week after school. Because she depends on that machine for survival, if the tube implanted in her chest collapses she must go for immediate surgery. This year she has had two surgeries and some other health-related problems that have caused her to miss school. In spite of all the missed school she has maintained a 4.3 grade point average.

In addition to these absences counted against her, she is in the orchestra and when she is required to miss other classes to rehearse for a concert, those absences are counted. Also, she was required to take a practice CollegeBoard Advanced Placement English Literature exam, so she missed four periods that day and those were counted against her. Because of Jessica's expertise in technology, she obtained a part-time job working for the San Carlos School District maintaining computers. This job is in conjunction with the work/study program at Carlmont and plans are being made to expand it next year. She was asked to speak before a group of Silicon Valley educators once and had to miss a half day of school, which was counted against her. (She represented Carlmont High School and the program so well that she gave the speech in San Mateo County two weeks ago and will be speaking at the San Mateo Office of Education Technology meeting on May 5 at 4:00 p.m.)

Last week I took Jessica to New York to the School Technology Conference, and that was two more days of absences (her only absences unrelated to health or school functions). Jessica's physics class went to Great America on Friday, but Jessica did NOT GO because she could not take the risk of missing more school and having her absence count against her in other classes. Whenever she can, she will decline school functions and school-related extracurricular activities so they won't count against her. What we cannot predict is her health from now until school is out. We have received letters this week indicating that she now has ten absences.

I understand that the attendance policy is intended, by various measures positive and punitive, to motivate class attendance. I can assure you no motivation is necessary in Jessica's case. She has, in fact, insisted on attending class many days when she justifiably should have stayed home ill.

Furthermore, in order to minimize school absences, we have insisted that the hospital provide dialysis after school despite the Ambulatory Care Unit's preference for doing it earlier in the day. Additionally, we have rejected appointments desired by Jessica's doctors in recent *weeks to do certain disease-related tests because these appointments are available only during school hours; we are postponing them until school is out for the summer.*

We believe her academic achievement, <u>which must be the ultimate objective of any attendance policy,</u> speaks for itself. <u>We neither ask for, nor do we desire, any special consideration regarding academic requirements</u>.

I am writing this to let you know the hardship the rigid application of this attendance policy is causing people like us. We believe ideally all students should be treated the same, but all students are not the same. We wish Jessica were the same as everyone else and did not have to depend on a machine and access to that machine for survival.

I believe your attendance policy is a good one, but it needs some revision to take into consideration individual special circumstances.

Thank you for your consideration of this matter.

But the notices continue. Eventually, some of my teachers are (to my parents' horror) driven to dishonesty on my behalf; my mom receives a call one evening after one of my catheter replacement surgeries from a teacher who tells her, "Just so you know—I marked Jessica as present today."

I end my junior year one absence short of fifteen in nearly all my classes and therefore avoid the penalty that would have crushed me. The next two semesters, I nearly crush myself as a high school senior intent on graduating with High Honors despite more dialysis troubles and the continuing unfair attendance policy. When my Calculus teacher tells me that I will not be allowed to make up tests that I miss, I am driven to leave the hospital after an early-morning surgery and rush to class, still recovering from general anesthesia and feeling tremendous pain. There is nothing more exhilarating than beating the school at its own game.

Shortly after my graduation in 1999, the district's policy is deemed illegal. Information published in the local newspaper states it concisely and clearly:

> *The Sequoia Union High School District will be fined $500 a day if it continues a policy under which students may be given 'no grade' marks and dropped from classes if they are absent too often. In a decision issued Thursday, U.S. District Judge Maxine Chesney ordered the district to start paying the daily fine on June 20 until it stops implementing this specific aspect of its attendance policy... The part of the policy the judge objected to says a student who meets minimum objectives for a class but attends class less than 60 hours a semester will receive a grade of 'NG,' meaning 'no grade.' In other words, a student can earn a B grade but will not receive it if the student misses too many classes... In 1989, a lawsuit by the group [Citizens LEAP] forced the district to end its attendance policy, but in July 1997, the district put the new one in place.*

It still fascinates me that the attendance policy was in effect precisely during my two years of dialysis. Even when I read of the policy's reversal, I am thankful for its existence during my junior and senior years, for without a doubt, it strengthened me. Good grades, I soon realize, are a fleeting and meaningless accomplishment, and my high school obsession was in error. But lessons learned in perseverance are forever.

I am sympathetic to the District's repeated attempts to motivate class attendance. But as any teacher knows, true motivation is intrinsic, not extrinsic, and enacting unreasonable punishments will not inspire greatness. My motivation to attend school comes from within, but life occasionally gets in the way. Even so, nothing can prevent me from learning.

ruminations from the rink

In an effort to rigidly adhere to a policy of equal treatment for all, my school discriminated against me. They used my classroom attendance record, which was just a number on a piece of paper, to apply a stereotype: in the eyes of the administration, I became an unmotivated student prone to truancy and in need of disciplinary action. (Strangely for a district so obsessed with data, the school ignored another number: my grade point average.)

I think that real danger rests in the removal of our own individuality. Unique circumstances and who a person really is cannot be accurately conveyed by a one-dimensional number. Although there were certainly those who would abuse the system, I wasn't one of them. In fact, it was in academics that I firmly (and erroneously) rested my self-worth. It is ironic, then, that the activity that I most wanted to pursue was the one that I was penalized for—on the grounds that I was not taking my education seriously.

To a lesser extent, there are other ways in which we daily forget to take individuality into account. I cannot count how many times I was told growing up that as someone with cystinosis, I should crave pickles and olives—two of my least favorites, then and now. Though told all patients should do one thing or take a particular pill or supplement, I cannot fathom how much damage it would have done to me personally to blindly heed all that advice only on the grounds that I have cystinosis.

On the other hand, generalizations and discrimination give us the chance to excel beyond expectations. Throughout elementary and middle school, my standardized test scores in math were generally good, but it wasn't until I heard that children with cystinosis had difficulties in mathematical processes that my test results moved into the ninety-ninth percentile starting in eighth grade. Likewise, although my early high school report card scores were in the A range, after being told that dialysis would lower my ability to concentrate and that I would experience a slippage in grades, I became driven to earn even higher marks across the gambit of an even more difficult course load. When told that I would receive no credit for classes from which I was excessively absent, I pulled out IVs after surgery and begged to be taken to school and got myself out of bed on days when I could have legitimately stayed home. Rather than fulfill the stereotype of a truant, I doubled my efforts to convince my teachers that I was one of the most motivated individuals ever to set foot in their classrooms. Although discrimination is never warranted, it can be used as impetus to drive us to break through the usual stereotypes.

Are you the victim of an unwanted stereotype or unfair discrimination? Turn your victimhood into empowerment, and remember, sometimes showing up is the first step to proving everyone wrong.

Rolling forward…

thirteen | remembering amnesia

Hope springs eternal in the human breast:
Man never Is, but always To be blest.

Alexander Pope

My eighteenth birthday comes and goes without incident. I assume, as I have for the past year or so, that the day will never come. Maybe the hospital has lost my number. Maybe I am just too far down on the kidney waiting list after all. Maybe they are all lies: the nephrology team tells me I am first to keep me from giving up hope and dying of disappointment. Of course, I am too stubborn to let something like dialysis determine my will to live. But somewhere, deep down, I have accepted dialysis as the very definition of keeping me alive. For the rest of my life. However long it might be.

My mom, at least outwardly, is more optimistic than I am. It is 1999 and we have just gotten cell phones to replace our pagers as the means by which we will learn that a kidney is ready for me. Upon leaving for work each morning, my mom tells my dad that she will have her phone nearby and on.

"Hope springs eternal!" she says on her way out every time she leaves the house. I get weary of the phrase, but thankfully, I do not know the second part of the famous Alexander Pope quotation.

When I am told to be especially "ready" on holiday weekends when the drunk drivers are out, it strikes me how very morbid the whole thing is anyway. Do I really want to think about waiting for someone to die? And so I live, dialysis treatment to dialysis treatment, Monday to Wednesday to Friday to Monday.

I always look forward to Dr. Alex's visits. He doesn't come every time, but I count on seeing him at least once every couple of weeks, and every time I have some sort of problem, such as a slow session. In hemodialysis, the blood needs to be processed at a particular flow rate in order to have an effective treatment. Because my dialysis catheters are always so problematic, I can rarely be dialyzed at optimal speed. Even with the largest filter available, the machine is not able to successfully remove toxins and normalize my levels when this issue exists. If the rate is slightly low, my session is just extended by an hour or two. If the rate is very low, I'm scheduled for another dialysis catheter placement surgery. So far, I have had seven replacements, and it seems that I will soon need another one.

Dr. Alex comes by one afternoon in late July, a couple weeks after my birthday. He tells me that through some loopholes, I am maintaining my position on the pediatric kidney list despite reaching legal adulthood. In theory, I know that this is preferable to being transitioned to the bottom of the much longer adult list. In my own emotional reality, though, this news isn't monumental. If being first on the pediatric list hasn't resulted in my liberation from the dialysis machine for the past twenty months, why would anything change now? Dialysis, in my mind, is perpetual. It keeps me alive. It grants me the opportunity to disobey dietary restrictions and burden my own barely functioning kidneys, because the large mechanical kidney can remove the toxins. For four mind-numbingly slow hours every Monday, Wednesday, and Friday, the machine makes me whole.

It also makes me feel like crap, but that is just par for the course.

This isn't to say that I don't maintain a normal life outside of my dialysis treatments. In fact, this summer, I continue to work the part-time technical support job that I have had since my junior year of high school, and I am able to accumulate more hours due to the absence of a rigorous high school schedule. My employer knows I am on dialysis, but I don't think he truly understands its impact on my life and how much pride I take in both being on dialysis and working for him in an industry that I love.

Perhaps it's the nature of being a teenager, but it is much more grudgingly that I volunteer to help with one of my mother's technology workshops. You see, my mom and I share many of the same loves, now and later in life:

teaching (specifically, junior high students), history, and technology. So it is only natural that my mom would be on the cutting edge of integrating technology and learning, and that she would lead sessions on how other educators can successfully blend the two. Whether I am more interested in asserting my independence or if I just don't want her to know I am fascinated by the things she is doing, I don't know. But for whatever reason, my willingness to help her out is always somewhat lacking. Nevertheless, this summer, I am her aide during a three-day workshop, and by today, the second day of the workshop, I am just starting to find my place in the room filled with computers and teachers.

I am unusually hungry at lunchtime, and I make my way down to the building's cafeteria to get myself a bite to eat. Being a dialysis patient often means that I have no appetite or desire for food, but Dr. Alex has recently put his foot down (again) on my dairy consumption. He tells me repeatedly that even the relatively small amount of milk I drink (compared to the gallon I used to consume daily) is poison to my kidneys. And my food and drink choices at home are pretty limited to whatever the family shopper decides to stock in the fridge. (This typically means non-dairy, high-calorie drinks for old people. Not that these drinks are for my parents. These drinks are purchased specifically for yours truly.) So today, I am famished. As I peruse the cafeteria menu, however, I realize the irony of being told— by my dietician, nurses, social worker, and doctor—that I need to get more calories while at the same time being given a long list of foods I must not eat and told to cooperate.

I ponder these injustices while eating my dry cafeteria sandwich, imagining how wonderful it would be to wash it down with a nice tall, cold glass of milk. I settle for orange juice and reluctantly return to my mom's classroom, awaiting the arrival of her teacher-students from their own lunches. When they arrive, my mom introduces their next assignment (to create a classroom website) and sets them to work. I do my job of wandering the room, asking teachers if they need help, and assisting them when they call me over. I hear my mom's cell phone ringing its usual *Ode to Joy* melody and observe her slip outside the room.

When she comes back in, she seems emotional. She simply says with a huge smile on her face, "This is it!" Everyone looks up, wondering what she is talking about.

I am afraid, excited, and unbelieving: for despite what I had assumed was a complete lack of hope on my part, I feel certain I know exactly what she is talking about.

I insist on going home to take a bath. As I sit in the tub, I wonder if this could possibly be my last time. I haven't been able to take a shower since getting my dialysis catheter placed nearly two years ago; because the area isn't supposed to get wet, washing my hair has been difficult (I've generally asked my mom to do it for me, since I have such a hard time getting the soap out when I lean my head over the sink) and feeling genuinely clean has been nearly impossible.

Nerves kick in. Of all the things that I worry about regarding the transplant, the drugs that will follow it present the most dread. I am particularly antagonistic to the idea of taking post-transplant steroids, which I associate with a puffy face and weight gain. It has happened countless times: one year I attend a cystinosis conference and a person looks perfectly normal. The next year, after that person has had a transplant, he has a rounded face. I don't want that for myself, though as I mindlessly rub my neck with a wash cloth I realize that a new life and freedom from dialysis should be more important than skin-deep vanity.

I hastily dry myself off, dress in comfortable sweats, and throw some clothes into a bag. We load up the car and I am heading to Stanford Hospital for life-changing surgery.

Once at the hospital and through the admission process, I am hastily greeted by the transplant coordinator before I am stripped of my clothing, covered in Betadine (I guess my cleansing bath wasn't so cleansing after all), given a loose hospital gown with one too many openings, and put into a wheelchair. Dr. Alex is unfortunately out of town. I am so angry with him that I vow to kill him when he returns. First I will hug him and toast him with the milk that I will be drinking without guilt, and then I will kill him.

Another doctor on the transplant team comes in with my first dose of immunosuppressants, the drugs that will prevent my body from treating the new kidney as a foreign object worthy of attack. She sits down with me and carefully goes over each one; there are a lot of pills for me to take. The dreaded steroid, prednisone, is there. Also present is one I immediately identify as particularly evil before it even goes into my mouth: cyclosporine. Those are some huge, smelly pills. There are no sedatives yet. I don't even have an IV at this point.

My lunchtime sandwich is discussed. Eating before surgery is not ideal, but I am told that the surgeon thinks it will be okay. The transplant team knows me, and no one tends to believe I really had all that much, anyway.

The nephrologist then tells me a little about the surgery. Because it is the longest procedure I have ever had, the anesthetics will be more intense than I am used to. She describes something she calls preoperative amnesia.

"The general anesthesia will be powerful enough," she explains, "that you won't remember what happened during the couple hours before surgery. You certainly won't recall this conversation."

Huh, interesting.

I call my youth pastor to tell him that I am about to be wheeled in for transplant surgery. He prays for me over the phone.

I am excited for the usual: the struggle to get an IV placed in a predictably uncooperative vein and the relief once it is in. The relaxing sedatives that will be given after I am transferred from wheelchair to gurney and before full-blown general anesthesia. A doctor in the operating room, preferably one with greying temples, who will place a mask over my nose and mouth and tell me to count backwards from ten. Hopefully before then I can take in my surroundings and—*is it possible?*—ask to see the kidney before the surgery begins!

But I sit parked in a wheelchair, waiting in a room after talking to my pastor on the phone. And then there is nothing.

ruminations from the rink

As you may have guessed, I remember no more of what happened on the day I had my kidney transplant.

What I do know, though, is that I wasn't the only one in a fog. Somewhere, outside of my own supportive and small network, a family was in shock.

When you get a call that an organ is available after many months (or even years) of waiting, you are told the exciting news that it's time for your body to be repaired, it's time for the 'restart' button to get a push, it's time for a new life.

The transplant coordinator doesn't call to say, "I regret to inform you that a young man was tragically killed last night."

But that's exactly what happened. In the early hours of August 12, 1999, while I was safe and sound in my bed dreaming all kinds of selfish dreams, a nineteen-year-old was killed in San Francisco in a drive-by shooting. I think about the terror and disbelief that must have gone through his mother's heart when she received a phone call less than twelve hours before I received mine. And yet, whether acting on his previously stated wishes or making her own difficult decision in those early minutes of heartbreak, she chose not to cling to her son's body but to offer it so that others might gain the second chance that he couldn't have. It is because of this choice that I am able to cling to Jesus.

Right about now you are probably thinking, *Hey, wait a second. I knew that this God thing was being weaved throughout this book, but I didn't realize I was going to get a sermon!*

Hear me out. This is my memoir, and you probably picked it up at least in part because you wanted to learn what goes through the head of someone who lives with a known killer every day of her life. And in the chaos of going to college, moving 300 miles away from home for my first job after graduating, deciding to switch my career to one in the field of education, getting married, dealing with my military husband's seven-month deployment to the Middle East, teaching junior high, working as dean of a school, educating doctors about a disease of which they know nothing, fighting with health insurance companies, learning that my own noncompliance has done irreversible damage that will claim my ability to verbally communicate, swallowing pills every six hours that make me throw up, trying to piece together a terrible sequence of events that ended with the murder of both of my husband's parents, and taking on each new thing that is unexpectedly thrown my way, there is only one thought that has consistently gone through my head every day of my life since August 12, 1999. And this is it:

Another person unknowingly made the ultimate sacrifice for me. **He died so that I may live.** I am so undeserving.

We are all so undeserving. We often lament that life is unfair, but in reality, if I were to really get what I deserve, I would experience much worse than I could possibly imagine—for all of eternity. My sin separates me from a perfect God.

Enter Jesus. Unlike my kidney donor, Jesus willingly died for me. And also unlike my kidney donor, Jesus knew (and knows) me in all my selfishness, all my avarice, all my jealousy, all my pride. He took my sins to the cross so that my soul could be repaired, my 'restart' button could get a push, and I could have a new and eternal life.

I don't know that I would think about this every day if not for my transplant. From sacrifice came life. A young man died for my body. A perfect Son of God died for my soul. And sometimes, when I'm driving home from work and thinking about the gifts I have been given, I start to cry tears of pure amazement, because my transplant story is my glimpse at the redemption story. "For God so loved the world that he gave his one and only Son, that whoever believes in him shall not perish but have eternal life" (John 3:16). He's calling. I hope you will answer, because he has some life-changing news.

Rolling forward…

fourteen | bulimia: controlling what is outside of our control

The diminutive chains of habit are seldom heavy enough to be felt till they are too strong to be broken.

Samuel Johnson

It is more important to know what kind of patient has the disease than what kind of disease the patient has.

Sir William Osler

It all starts with a sloppy joe.

My move from the Intensive Care Unit to the regular transplant floor is delayed because there is no room in the inn. Or at least, that is what I am told.

"We keep trying to get you out of here," the nurse tells me, "but there are no beds available."

✧ ✧ ✧ ✧ ✧

When I first wake up from the transplant surgery, I have a breathing tube down my throat that is immensely uncomfortable. A glance at the clock reveals that it is 3:00 a.m. I bang on the side of the bed until a nurse comes in. After gesturing for a pen and paper, I write ominously, "If this tube doesn't come out of my throat, I am going to die." (No, I'm not a dramatic person at all. Really.)

When it is finally removed, I collapse a lung and am made to use a breathing exerciser three times a day. With a collapsed lung, breathing hurts. The last thing I want to do is force deep breaths. Clearing my throat and coughing are also very painful, but unsurprisingly (because isn't this just how the world works?), they are as necessary as they are painful. Whatever adult happens to be in the room (my mom, my dad, or a nurse) holds a pillow against my new kidney whenever I say I need to cough. It feels a bit better that way.

I don't know if my collapsed lung, my self-labeled near-death experience (I leap off the bed the first morning while in some sort of drug-induced stupor, convinced of my own impending doom), my difficulty with pain management, or the sleeping kidney (wake up and work, already!) have anything to do with my extended sojourn in the ICU. When told that there are no beds available on the hospital floor, I do decide to give the nurse the benefit of the doubt.

A push-button remote is given to me. It is gloriously attached to an IV bag with morphine in it. Oh, what fun it is to push that button!

One of the nurses observes my behavior with alarm. The engage-at-will, push-button remote is replaced with a similar looking device with a timer. I can no longer push the button more than once in a half-hour period. I watch the clock and push the button every half hour.

The remote is taken away from me. It is explained that I will no longer have any control over the morphine. (I silently wonder, *Do I have an addictive personality?*)

No one really explains to me, though, why I am not allowed to have real food while in the ICU. (But it's to be expected. I've already learned from the morphine incident that ICU stands for *Intent on Crushing Überbliss.*) I am given apple juice and a very tasteless gelatin. It is my first hint that perhaps something about myself has fundamentally changed: I am obsessed with the idea of getting food in my belly.

Finally, I am moved to hospital wing Two North. And then it arrives. A build-your-own sloppy joe meal.

Because my transfer takes place mid-morning, I don't get to select my lunch. I am given the default fare.

But it is the best-tasting food I have ever eaten—rather, devoured—in my life. I am so sad that there isn't more of it. I don't think I've ever had a sloppy joe. Why have I never had a sloppy joe before? Why hasn't anyone told me how good this is?

Over the next few weeks, I learn that there is, sadly, nothing special about a sloppy joe after all. I just happen to really enjoy and crave food for perhaps the first time in my life. But when I look in the mirror, I am greeted by a prednisone face, and I know that my own appetite has to be controlled.

For as long as I can remember, my number one concern about transplant has been the effects of the steroids designed to prevent rejection. Prednisone, used as a treatment after my transplant and for transplants for decades prior, can cause fat pockets to develop in odd places: in the jowls, on the back, and in other just generally unattractive locations. Prednisone itself does not create fat, of course—but it does increase appetite. And once a person on high prednisone doses starts consuming food, the fat gets put in these new, undesirable places. Such a person might be identifiable by his or her so-called prednisone "moon face."

I am horrified when I see the moon face.

And my horror increases exponentially when I read Wayne's letters to me during my recovery period: after several months in Virginia, his family will be returning to California at the end of November.

My determination is extreme. I deny myself fatty foods despite intense hunger. Behind my own closed bedroom door, I spend more than an hour each evening walking or even jogging in place. I will be the exception. I will not gain weight after my transplant, and once I lose enough weight, surely I will start losing it from my face. When Wayne sees me, I will look normal.

Unfortunately, I have a major complication after my transplant. Once the kidney does "wake up" and an initial bout of nephrotoxicity-fueled acute rejection is discovered through a biopsy and subsequently reversed (with a simple change in immunosuppressant therapy from cyclosporine to tacrolimus), my transplant team struggles to find the root cause of a troubling symptom: I am retaining large amounts of fluid. It was always expected that the transplant would remedy my Fanconi syndrome and I would no longer experience excessive thirst or urination, but now I am hardly urinating at all. I am put on high doses of diuretics, and in an effort to monitor and control my situation, Dr. Alex tells me to start weighing myself twice a day.

My diagnosis, which will go on to stump doctors and heavily impact my quality of life, is Superior Vena Cava Syndrome. It is discovered via ultrasound that when my dialysis catheter was removed after transplant, the main vein into my heart collapsed under the pressure of scar tissue that had formed as a result of my multiple catheter replacements over two years. Perhaps the Inferior Vena Cava will grow to compensate; in the mean time, diuretics and daily weighings will continue to be a part of my routine.

I am already obsessed with my post-transplant weight owing to years of built-up fear over becoming chubby due to the drugs. Vanity is queen in the face of the anticipation surrounding the return of the love of my life. And now, I am given not only a dangerous habit to follow—the weighing of myself every morning and evening—but I am also given the means to decrease the number that appears when I step on the scale. I discover that taking my prescribed diuretic, a 40 milligram furosemide tablet, can result in the loss of as much as five pounds in a twenty-four hour period. That this is water weight, and not real weight, matters little to me.

Just before my transplant, my charted dialysis dry weight was 48.0 kilograms, or 105.6 pounds. Now, just three months later in early November 1999, a post-transplant appointment has me weighing in at 42.6 kilograms, or 93.7 pounds. Dr. Alex adds a diagnosis of *anorexia* into his clinic report and I am told that I have two weeks to gain weight or else I'll be admitted to the hospital.

Meanwhile, I continue to weigh myself excessively (doctor's orders), take a prescribed diuretic (sometimes two), and obsess over what I put in my mouth and how many steps walked in private it will take to work those calories off. On the morning of my next appointment a fortnight later, I know I have lost more weight.

I frantically search my room for something to weigh me down and am thankful that I have been collecting pennies for as long as I can remember. I tie baggies of pennies around each leg and at the belt line inside my loose jeans. I attach a tall, cylindrical coin bank to my stomach and put on a large sweatshirt to hide the extra bulk.

I weigh in at 43.2 kilograms. Everyone seems satisfied, and I feel ready to reunite with Wayne. When I convince Dr. Alex to taper my prednisone dose and eventually remove it from my regimen entirely, I feel a sense of victory on all fronts.

I received my transplant three days before move-in day at the University of California, Berkeley. While I had been prepared to live in the dorms and commute to dialysis three times a week, my transplant requires taking a semester off. This does not work in my favor, however necessary: I think downtime lends itself to obsessive behaviors and bad habits. But when I finally start at Berkeley in January 2000, there is little need for me to maintain my secret exercise habits. I obtain housing in a dormitory at the top of a hill on the north end of campus and daily make several hikes up and down that hill to attend classes, meet friends at Sproul Plaza on the south side, or eat at one of several dining halls. For the time being, I stop my paranoid weighing habits and discontinue denying myself food. In fact, there are days when I binge on a whole box of my favorite organic cookies or an entire bag of heavily sweetened dried pineapple.

But my fluid retention issues have not been resolved, and I feel certain that I am waking up feeling more and more puffy as time goes on. I finally receive a useful (and ultimately, detrimental) piece of information from a transplant clinic nurse at a routine appointment.

"Your body can adjust a bit to a diuretic when you take it daily," she tells me when I lament having to limit my fluid intake even when I am thirsty. "We may need to increase your dose a bit simply because it has become ineffective at the current number of milligrams."

She doesn't know that I'm already taking two, and sometimes three, times the prescribed amount. But now I start pushing my body to go a day or two without diuretics, then take five or six times what I'm supposed to. I find by returning to the scale at home during my school's Spring Break that this can result in a ten-pound weight loss overnight.

When several venoplasties and the stenting of my Superior Vena Cava do not alleviate my fluid retention woes, I continue to abuse my furosemide throughout college. I feel relatively healthy, but with my new-found independence and freedom has come new cysteamine noncompliance (I do not take a single dose of Cystagon while at Berkeley) and prescription drug addiction. My eating habits catch up with me in my sophomore year, and although I avoided gaining the "Freshman Fifteen," I somehow manage to put on the sophomore thirty. As soon as I realize what has happened (because the weight truly seems to appear overnight!), it increases my desperation for diuretics. When I am unable to get furosemide refills quickly enough, I look into alternative—and less legal—ways of obtaining the medicine. Upon moving out of the dorms and into an apartment with body-conscious (but not weight-obsessed) roommates, a scale returns to the bathroom for twice-daily weighings. I have taken my freedom and made myself a slave to my own body image.

Fast forward to 2004. I have just accepted my first full-time, permanent job, working as a Writer/Editor in the World Geography department of an educational publishing company, where I will be responsible for issues pertaining to the Middle East. It seems miraculous that I have found a job in my field of study, which ultimately ended up being Middle Eastern history, politics, culture, religion, and language.

It is a relief to be moving away. As many university graduates experience, I have felt recently that my return to my parents' home represents a regression after my college independence. It is a long five months between graduation and getting a job offer, though I work as a part-time desktop support person within my former elementary school district while searching for a career. Relocating several hundred miles away to beautiful, coastal Santa Barbara feels like a dream come true.

I respond to an advertisement in a church bulletin for a room for rent in the house of a middle-aged Christian woman; I feel too overwhelmed with the unfamiliarity of the situation to search for my own place. And for the location—between downtown and the beach—her rates are extremely reasonable.

From the very beginning, I am somewhat uncomfortable in the house, but I know that I will have to receive a few paychecks before I can afford the first- and last-months' rent required as a deposit at most of the studio apartments in Santa Barbara.

The house has rooms for four tenets, and the owner struggles to keep any of them (save mine) filled for more than one month, in part due to her own missteps in landlordship. Several housemates come and go, lured in by the inexpensive rent but then eager to escape the tight control that prevents them from talking above a whisper after 6:00 p.m., cooking in the kitchen, or seeing an explanation for the money they are charged for utilities.

After about two months in the house, a new, naïve tenet moves in. Jamie is full of life and I like her immediately. She has a smile and enthusiasm that are contagious; she is a young nineteen-year-old (I am twenty-three) pursuing a psychology degree at the local community college. She, however, is not a local resident and has moved from the East Coast to Santa Barbara purely for the excitement of the unknown. If everyone has a story, Jamie's sounds like it will be full of plot twists and adventure.

Strange things occur, though, with Jamie's arrival. Food from the kitchen starts disappearing and reappearing; Jamie give excuses such as the one she gives me this evening.

"I was out of cereal this morning so I used yours after you left for work, but I bought you a new box."

"Thanks, but I don't mind if you eat a bowl of my cereal if you run out. You didn't need to buy a whole new box. What I had was nearly new. Where is the opened box?" I am worried that she has perhaps juxtaposed the owner's possessive nature regarding items in the kitchen (including pots and pans and appliances) with my own, and feels that even touching my stuff demands full replacement.

"Oh. Well, see, I left for school in a rush this morning, but I was hungry. I wanted to grab a bowl, but you know how Sheila feels about dishware leaving her house. So I grabbed the whole box. After I ate some in a paper cup in my car, I threw the box in the back seat. I came to a sudden stop later on the highway because I was daydreaming one minute and the next minute I was about to hit the car in front of me. The cereal went everywhere. I didn't want to give you back cereal that had spilled all over my car, because you know how dirty my car is! So I bought you a new box."

Her story feels exhausting and defensive, but I don't question it.

In the days to come, there are other such stories; she seems to divide her food theft between myself and our other two housemates fairly equally, such that one of us might have a single item go missing once a week.

Another strange occurrence is the speed at which we start going through toilet paper upon Jamie's arrival. Whereas we had previously been buying it only infrequently, it now feels that every weekend a trip to the store for another super-size package is required. My other two housemates at the time start to grumble.

"It's not our fault the new girl has bowel problems," one says to me. "She should be responsible for buying the toilet paper for our bathroom from now on."

I don't like that when Jamie isn't home, the conversation seems to drift to her very private business. It seems more appropriate to confront her directly about the issue.

I softly knock on her door. "Jamie?" I call.

"Come in, Jess," she says. I find her with her textbooks open in front of her and her laptop balanced on her knee. I sit on the floor across from her.

"Wow, your room is a lot warmer than mine," I say. With winter approaching, I am even more disheartened by the broken window next to my bed that Sheila has said she won't fix. It makes me uncomfortably cold at night, even after constructing a makeshift closure with a worn-out pair of jeans and some duct tape. (Not to mention the fact that I am convinced a deadly spider will crawl up my nose any day now.)

"This is so useless!" Jamie suddenly exclaims, throwing her hands up in the air before setting her laptop aside. "Why bother with school if you're only taught pointless facts?"

I smile and shrug. At this moment, I am very glad that college is behind me.

We make small talk for a while, taking on the injustices of the collegiate experience and the problems with men. Finally, I shift to the subject that seems so difficult to broach.

"Jaime, are you feeling okay these days? I am worried about you. I know this is pretty personal, but you seem to go through a lot of toilet paper. I just want to know that you are okay."

She is quiet for a long time. Because I sense that her silence is due to a careful consideration of her answer, and not because I have offended her, I continue to sit with her. Like Socrates, she ends up wisely answering my question with a question.

"Jess, have you ever encountered something seemingly insurmountable? Something that you hate about yourself, but something you feel powerless to change?"

"Hmmm. I think so. Are you talking about a physical trait or condition or something like that? Or an action?"

"Both, I think."

"Well, I've always hated my upper arms. They're so manly! And I hate that it seems impossible for me to be able to set aside the twenty minutes three times a week that it would take to change them." I don't know her too well, so of course I am not revealing too much of myself. Plus, my diuretic addiction is, by this point, so second nature that it doesn't even occur to me that I have a serious problem.

She smiles weakly. Clearly, my upper arms present no comparison to what she is about to share with me. "Can I tell you something? I mean, something really serious?"

"Of course."

And with that, I learn that Jamie lives with bulimia. This petite young woman, probably no more than ninety pounds, binges on food and then purges it out of her system. I value the time Jamie takes to educate me about the subject. She does have a stereotypical characteristic of anorexia in that when she looks into the mirror, she sees obesity. However, her condition is also marked by overeating and the inability to control herself around food, traits of bulimia.

"The reason for the toilet paper is that I am also obsessive-compulsive when it comes to bathroom cleanliness. If even a drop of vomit were to get on the toilet seat, I would have to get on my hands and knees and scrub the whole bathroom. Therefore, I line the toilet with several layers of paper before purging."

I nod and search cautiously for the words to say. I feel neither disgusted nor judgmental, and I want to make sure I don't convey these emotions through careless words.

"Jamie," I start slowly, "you *know* you wear size zero in women's clothing. You *know* in your head that you don't weigh much. Why do you think your rational knowledge and emotional feelings are so disconnected?"

"I think, Jess, that it has more to do with prevention. Most of the women in my family are overweight. You're right; in my head, I know that I am not fat. In my head, I even believe that I could stand to gain ten pounds! But in my heart, that is a slippery slope, and if I gain even half a pound, I am destined to gain fifty. I believe weight gain is my fate, and in order to overcome such a strong fate, I have to take strong measures."

"Okay. Worst-case scenario. Say you *do* gain fifty pounds, which doesn't seem likely to me with reasonable eating and regular exercise. Is it better to carry that extra weight or be dead?"

Her long sigh and heartbreaking response don't surprise me. "I wish I could say the right answer. Because I know the right answer to that question. But I'm so adamantly opposed to being heavy that I'd rather die skinny and attractive than live on after gaining that kind of weight. Plus, you're forgetting that the worst-case scenario that you consider improbable is much more likely for a person who binges."

We sit in silence for a while. Finally I say, "Do you think bulimia is who you are?"

"Not necessarily, but I do think it's *inseparable* from who I am. I wouldn't describe myself as 'the bulimic,' but I would say that I'm 'Jamie with bulimia.' It dictates my actions more than college, more than relationships, more than career aspirations, more than my thirst for adventure and desire for not only world peace, but peace within my own family. Bulimia comes first." She pulls out a book from underneath her bed. It is about the psychology of bulimia. "Are you really interested?"

"Yes." I take the book and open it. And there we sit, well past midnight, with me reading a book on bulimia and Jamie reluctantly propping her computer back on her knee and resuming her term paper. When my eyelids get heavy, I go to my room, get my pillow and blanket, and return to spread out on Jamie's floor. I doze to the sound of her manicured nails on the computer keyboard. Though I have always hated that sound, for some reason, it doesn't bother me tonight. There are far worse sounds. Like the sound of someone destroying her life over a toilet bowl.

At one point, she gets up and makes a move toward the hallway. "Where are you going?" I ask, immediately alert.

"I'm going to the bathroom. But I haven't had anything to eat today, so you don't need to worry."

And so begins life with Jamie. Our verbal exchanges range from the serious (trusting God with her weight) to the silly *(don't touch my Cheerios! I spent my measly dollar-an-hour salary on those and I don't want a half a day's work to end up in the toilet!)* to the everyday mundane. I try hard to not see myself as an enabler when I accompany Jamie on weekly toilet paper runs after a house meeting ends with the decision that she should be in charge of purchasing paper goods for the bathroom. (In order to limit her shame, the other two unknowing housemates—who assume Jamie has some sort of serious bowel disorder—have divided up the household work and purchases based on area of the house. Jamie seems to randomly get the bathroom.)

As for the beautiful qualities that I had originally sensed in my newest housemate, they are all still there. She is not a bulimic. She is Jamie with bulimia, and I pray every day for that *with* to become a *without*.

In 2007, Santa Barbara is a distant memory and I have long since devoted my life to teaching junior high. Wayne watches as I line up fifteen furosemide tablets on the counter in front of me and begin to swallow them dry, one by one.

"Do you always take that many?" He isn't sure. Living with me is still so new.

"Only about every three days," I answer. I carefully put the bottle back with my other medications in the cabinet. No need to highlight the fact that the prescription label reads *Take one tablet daily* just yet.

ruminations from the rink

I have always had a complicated relationship with food. Because it was so difficult to get me interested in eating during my pre-transplant years, I was understandably allowed anything I asked for. If I wanted to eat ten hotdogs in one sitting or a whole family pack of cool ranch tortilla chips, everyone was overjoyed.

I therefore didn't have a very strong concept of healthy eating or moderation. As was evidenced by my morphine incident in the ICU immediately following my transplant, I am perhaps prone to addictive behavior. With all the factors that contributed to how I viewed my post-transplant weight—the long-term concern of becoming heavy due to the drugs, the moon face I desperately wanted to get rid of, the fluid retention that mandated twice-daily weighings, the diuretics that made a one-dimensional number (my weight) decrease, and my fear of not being accepted by a teenage boy—coupled with my propensity for addictive behavior and my ignorance of healthy eating, it is not surprising that things fell into place for me to develop what my doctor casually labeled as anorexia. (In reality, the purging characteristic of bulimia can be done via laxatives, *diuretics,* or self-induced vomiting. But denying myself food and exercising off every calorie just after transplant may have indicated anorexia. I think my case was complicated and I am not qualified to diagnose it in hindsight.)

The hypocrisy of me playing the counselor five years later when I learned of Jamie's bulimia is not something that haunts me at night, because I recognize now that at that time and for several years afterward, I hadn't yet acknowledged my own destructive actions. Because of my desire to help her, the listening ear I offered Jamie allowed me to learn an important lesson that I carry with me to this day: we are all people first, and should not be labeled by our condition. For if we label ourselves as *the bulimic* or *the anorexic* or *the alcoholic* or *the diabetic* or *the cystinotic,* we have permitted our conditions to rule over us.

But we do need to acknowledge that our conditions exist. I greatly admired Jamie's willingness to share with me that she was *Jamie with bulimia.* Although I don't know where she is now, I imagine that she has been able to seek help and break free of her self-destruction.

I want to be very careful with the paradox here. I do believe that there are certain conditions that are outside of our *own* control; however, **uncontrollable impulses, addictions, diseases, and thoughts can be conquered.** It's just not something we can do on our own. Controlling the uncontrollable requires a wake-up call and outside help. For me, as you will soon find out, this meant a ride in an ambulance and a lot of prayer and support.

Rolling forward…

fifteen | the poisonous cure

Remedies often make diseases worse... It takes a wise doctor to know when not to prescribe.

Baltasar Gracián

I have a bad habit of telling doctors exactly what I need, sometimes to my detriment. I self-diagnose, then show up at my doctor's office to ask for the treatment for my specific, pre-determined issue.

My issues with fluid retention are not going away. My body has become so accustomed to furosemide that it is next to useless without managing for a period of time (usually three days) without it and then taking a much higher-than-recommended dose. By the time three days have passed, however, I am typically ten pounds heavier than I was on the first day of the cycle. (My twice-a-day weighing practice continues, nearly ten years after it first started.) I know I am abusing diuretics and I want to stop, but no physician seems to be able to offer a solution. No one is sure why I retain what I drink; it seems possible that even with my Superior Vena Cava unoccluded by way of stenting, upper-body scar tissue from my time on dialysis is still interfering with the overall flow of things in my system.

(Remember also that I lived the first eighteen years of my life with Fanconi syndrome and the excessive thirst that comes with it. It is excruciatingly hard to deny myself water or milk when I am thirsty. This issue feels to be the most terrible health situation I have had to deal with.)

With my diuretic becoming less effective seemingly by the day, I decide to demand new treatment. Perhaps mild fluid retention doesn't seem like an issue warranting attention, but my retention is severe, especially in the summer. Cystinosis can impair the ability of sweat glands to function properly, and in my case, I don't sweat. Without a built-in cooling mechanism, my body can overheat quite easily. On a hot day, my only alleviation is to drink cold water. Yet my retention is so formidable that when I drink what I feel like I need, I end up also needing to prop my head up on several pillows at night and can still find myself gasping for air under the pressure of excess upper-body fluid.

I cannot face another summer. Now being seen at a military hospital in a suburb of San Diego, I enter my doctor's office in early May. "My fluid retention has become unbearable," I tell him, "and I need another prescription to deal with it." My demanding demeanor at its best.

He draws me a diagram of how diuretics work. It all makes sense; my current diuretic is working in the loop of Henle, and if he gives me one that works in another part of the kidney, I will have double the fluid-draining power when taking the two together. I have some concerns, though. I know my current diuretic, furosemide, is potassium-depleting; I ask if this new diuretic is as well.

"No," my doctor reassures me. "Because it targets a different part of the kidney, it will not affect your potassium. It's one of the reasons that this medication is so safe to take in conjunction with what you already have."

And like a fool I believe him.

I return home with my newly filled prescription, and that evening take my first dose of metolazone along with my regular (as prescribed!) evening dose of furosemide. The next morning, I eagerly hop on the scale, and am surprised to find that I have dropped nearly five pounds of fluid. Certain this must be about all I have on me, I hesitate slightly before taking my morning regimen as delineated by my doctor. But since he had emphasized the importance of taking a low *maintenance dose* rather than going days without a diuretic and then shocking my system, I figure I might as well give it a try.

That evening, I say to my husband, "This drug is too good to be true. I feel great, but mark my words: *it is too good to be true.*"

And I do feel great. But by the following morning, the premonitions have kicked into high gear. I write my mom a quick e-mail.

Mom, I am having problems with the new drug I am on, metolazone. It is working. It is doing exactly what it is supposed to do, and it is doing it better than furosemide. It is a tiny dose and after taking half a pill in the morning I can drink and go to the bathroom at regular intervals all day. However, something seems wrong. I don't know how to explain it. Maybe it is just adjusting to a new drug and after ten years of fluid struggles finally having some normalcy. But I have this gut instinct that something is very wrong. I am trying to contact my doctor's office this morning to tell him that something is wrong.

I watch the clock following my early arrival at my editor's desk at work and call as soon as I know my doctor should be in. He tells me to cut my dose in half (down to a quarter of an already tiny pill) and call him back in a month. Apparently, my concerns are not high on his priority list.

I proceed to do what I should have done before ever popping the first pill: I conduct a quick Web search. Lo and behold, the medication that my doctor has told me is potassium-sparing is actually potassium-depleting. I sigh at the ignorance of some physicians, shake my head, and resume my work duties.

My husband, who has the day off, comes by mid-morning to share a snack with me in my office building's café. "I don't feel right," I tell him. "Maybe my blood sugar level is low. I'd better eat something sweet." A small cup of strawberries later, I feel fine. Even so, Wayne seems reluctant to leave.

"Do you want to have lunch in a little bit? How are you feeling?"

"I feel fine. Don't worry about me. It must have been my blood sugar. I need to get some work done, but if you want to stay close, I'll call you when I'm ready for lunch."

It isn't long before I feel odd. I can't focus well on my work and my brain seems to be swimming in my skull. I sense that I need to splash cold water on my face, throw up, or both. I push on, trying hard to focus on my computer screen. A wave of nausea comes over me, and I realize that I have to halt my stubborn attempts at toughness. I rise from my chair quickly (my first mistake) and rush out of the office. Once in the hallway, I eye my final destination—the bathroom—with urgency. Visions of my fifth grade Sunday School nightmare rush through my head: never again do I want to throw up publicly. It is essential that I make it to the toilet in time.

And then: nothing coherent. I briefly consider how lovely it would be to take a nap. Right now. I hear a distant thud, but am unaware that it came from my own head hitting the floor. In the blackness, all I can think about is sleeping soundly with not a care in the world.

"Jessica. Jessica? Can you hear me? Jessica?" I become vaguely aware that someone is trying to interrupt my sleep. I try hard to tune the annoying voice out. Why does she want to disturb me? "Oh my gosh. Jessica!" I feel someone take my arm and shake it gently. I open my eyes and see one of my coworkers leaning over me, her face creased with worry.

Oh my gosh, indeed. I close my eyes in horror when I realize where I am. In the hallway, on the way to the bathroom, I have collapsed. I am literally lying sprawled across the floor. I can't decide which is more humiliating: throwing up in front of my peers when I was ten or being discovered on the floor by my coworkers when I am twenty-seven.

I know I have to face reality sooner or later, so I respond to my coworker. "I fainted," I tell her, "but I'm fine now." I know I'm not fine, but it seems like the most appropriate thing to say to bring my embarrassment to a speedy end.

"Someone is calling 911," she informs me. I sigh heavily and pull myself up to a sitting position. *Great.*

The paramedics arrive with remarkable speed, and my husband, also nearby, is soon by my side as well. After a series of relatively superficial tests, the paramedics recommend a trip to the hospital.

When I ask if my husband can take me, the paramedics suggest against it. They believe that I best travel with them, so that they can monitor my heart rate and blood pressure and put me on IV fluids. When the words "cardiac arrest" are tossed around, I decide to heed their advice.

And so, for the first time in my life, I am placed in the back of an ambulance on a stretcher.

I have never entered an emergency room through the ambulance entrance, but on this day at Naval Medical Center San Diego, I learn that being dangerously ill definitely offers some advantages. Forget the waiting room, the triage process, and the long lulls between seeing any medical staff personnel at all. I am quickly wheeled into a private room and my blood is drawn in record speed. I feel myself drifting in and out of consciousness, or maybe I am just extremely tired. Either way, it seems that only five minutes have passed before a kind-looking, serious-faced gentleman in a white physician's coat and with clipboard in hand enters the room.

"Hello. You probably aren't feeling very chipper right now, are you?"

"Uh… no, not really. I'm pretty sleepy. Am I getting a sedative in my IV?"

He explains that I'm only receiving hydration fluids, but that blood tests have indicated that I am in an immediate and severe need of potassium. He is surprised I didn't go into cardiac arrest with my level as low as it is.

I audibly sigh. "My doctor told me metolazone wasn't potassium-depleting," I mumble, ashamed of myself for blindly trusting like I did. "I saw on the Internet this morning that it is. But I've been taking it for three days."

"Yes," the ER doctor tells me, "the metolazone and furosemide combination is extremely potent, and it sounds like you were put on essentially toxic doses."

ruminations from the rink

Because I have such a rare condition, I have learned to be my own advocate, educate physicians, and fight for what I need. As an adult, I have come to approach most doctors with suspicion, despite the fact that I was so well cared for as a child. In addition to knowing my body better than anyone else, I do know my medical needs fairly well.

Desperation can cloud common sense, though, and the irony is that my aggressive approach to ensuring that I get the best care (in my mind) can sometimes lead to poor decisions.

In one of my life's greatest paradoxes, however, this incident—in which ER doctors were amazed that I hadn't gone into cardiac arrest—served to heal me of my addiction to diuretics and the scale. Even though I would certainly never try the furosemide/metolazone combination again, I was also scared to realize just what damage could be done by taking diuretics. Taking ten or fifteen times my prescribed dose of furosemide suddenly seemed ridiculous at best, life threatening at worst. **From poison came healing.**

My struggles with fluid retention have not gone away, but I have been able to effectively deal with them using dietary methods and a small, *single* dose of furosemide as needed. I am not a slave to the scale, and as long as my clothes fit, I don't worry about whether I have gained a few pounds of either water weight or real weight.

Rolling forward...

sixteen | judgment

I am climbing the outside stairs to the center entrance to Wheeler Hall, where my second-year Arabic class is held. I am sleepy. Enrollment at Berkeley takes place in phases in order to maximize the likelihood of students getting into their most necessary subjects, and I am always torn about whether to sign up for Arabic in the first or second round. On the one hand, I assume that there is no possibility of my second-year Arabic class filling up—even in a post-September 11, 2001 world, most students are limiting their Arabic studies to one year. On the other hand, Arabic is required for my major, and if it were to fill up, my graduation might be delayed.

Switching my major last year from Electrical Engineering and Computer Science to Middle Eastern Studies was a huge decision. But I had decided to put aside what others might think of me, stymie my chances at earning six digits, and acknowledge that although I have a love for all things technical, I don't want any of the jobs that reside at the end of that road. There is no doubt that the career opportunities for Middle Eastern Studies majors are far fewer, but whatever those opportunities are (right now I'm not quite sure), I know that with them lies more of a chance that I will live out my passion. And if there is anything I am sure of, it is that I want to passionately live.

I don't know that passionate living includes early morning classes, however. This semester I had decided to take a risk and signed up for Arabic in the second round of TeleBears, Berkeley's automated enrollment system. Sure enough, there had still been room for me. But all the late-day classes were at capacity, leaving me to fight with my own weariness at 8:00 a.m. five times a week. Though an early riser, I don't think the college lifestyle takes kindly to such things.

I silently curse my decision to save Arabic for late registration as I enter Wheeler. The large auditorium—the one used for Friday night first-come, first-serve cheap movies—is directly in front of me. I veer left to the hallway lined with classrooms.

I see an able-bodied student patiently waiting for the elevator. I think I gawk a bit. Someone is using the elevator? In Wheeler Hall? How ludicrous. The building only comprises two functional floors and the ceiling is low. To avoid the shallow-step staircases that flank the auditorium is unheard of. *Lazy*, I think to myself. *She is entirely lazy.*

As I sink into my seat in the Arabic classroom, the guilt rises up within me almost immediately.

"As-salaam 'alaykum," my instructor says to me.

I reply weakly, "Wa 'alaykum as-salaam. Kayfa taqoulu kalimat *hypocrisy* bil 'arabiyah?" *What's the Arabic word for* hypocrisy?

My coworker and I are going out for burgers after a late-night editing session at the office. She is excited to introduce me to a place in downtown Santa Barbara where apparently you are given a bowl of ranch dressing in which to dip your hamburger. It is odd to see her get so excited about this; even growing up as part of a rare disease community in which eating ranch dressing straight up is completely normal (I've even done it myself), I've never known someone to so eagerly anticipate the opportunity. (And in my post-Fanconi adulthood, the very idea strikes me as kind of gross.)

Kelly knows about cystinosis. I told her about its existence several weeks ago, and being that both of us work in research-laden positions, it wasn't too surprising to me that she looked it up and took the time to learn about it. I have generally stopped caring about whether or not people know of my disease. But tonight Kelly reminds me why I used to find it hugely preferable that people not know.

"I have this terrible cold," she tells me. Really, she is stating the obvious. I have heard her sniffling from her cubicle all day, and I felt terrible that both of us were asked to stay late. She should have gone home and gotten some rest.

"Does it typically take you a long time to get over a cold?" I sincerely hope the answer is no. She sounds miserable, and even the ranch-dipped burger she holds in her hand isn't helping.

"Yes," she groans, "my colds seem to last forever! And when it rains, it pours. Sometimes a simple cold seems to usher in a migraine or the flu. Ugh, I just want to stay at home and sleep all day."

I hurt for her.

A few minutes pass with us silently chewing. Suddenly, she jerks upright on her bar stool.

"Oh my *gosh,* Jessica, I'm *so* sorry. I should *not* be talking about this cold. You have it *so* much worse. I have no right to complain. It's just a cold."

Funny, it never occurs to me that she has *just* a cold. In fact, it seems as though her cold has put her in more pain than most things I've experienced. I don't understand her assumption that I have it worse.

I sleep for much of the flight to Paris. I have been placed in First Class, a luxury that is lost on me (for I believe it was my sister who once told me that if the plane goes down, the people with the highest chance of survival are those seated behind the wings). I am in an aisle seat, and the man across from me has a prosthetic leg that he stretches out into the aisle. In my brief periods of alertness, I find myself wondering why he doesn't just take it off so he won't have to move it every time the stewardess walks by. I wonder if he feels shame and thinks it is better to have a fake leg rather than no leg at all, for the sake of keeping up appearances and preventing people from gaping at the void. I want to tell him that I don't mind if he wants to take his leg off. That like him, I am incomplete and my body broken. *What makes us unique helps make our spirits whole,* I think to myself. *We are all God's special creation. It's a shame that it's so easy to forget.*

ruminations from the rink

You may well be asking yourself: what is the paradox of judgment?

All of us do it. Not a single one of us is qualified to do so. **And more often than not, the very characteristic we are judging in someone else is one that we ourselves are, or have been, guilty of.** What made me so sick with disgust when I sat down in my Arabic class that day was that I knew that I myself was living with an invisible illness. Hastily and naturally, I had judged someone as lazy when I had no idea of her circumstances. *Nothing is wrong with that girl,* I thought. *She just doesn't want to walk!* What on earth gives me the right to determine what is going on with a person's physical and emotional wellbeing with one snooty glance?

My coworker, though well-meaning, also made a judgment call. She wrongly assumed that because I have experienced a great deal of serious health issues in my lifetime, I could only resent her for complaining about a common cold. In reality, if there's anything that my medical history has taught me, it's that there is nothing painful about the routine or expected—be it a dialysis routine, an anticipated kidney transplant, or a daily medication regimen exceeding, at one time, fifty pills. No, it is that which we are unprepared to handle—such as a summer cold that leaves us miserable—that is most difficult to take.

We also tend to extend grace to ourselves but not to others. Gretchen Rubin describes this scenario perfectly in *The Happiness Project:* "The 'fundamental attribution error' is a psychological phenomenon in which we tend to view other people's actions as reflections of their characters and to overlook the power of situation to influence their actions, whereas with ourselves, we recognize the pressures of circumstance. When other people's cell phones ring during a movie, it's because they're inconsiderate boors; if my cell phone rings during a movie, it's because I need to be able to take a call from the babysitter" (p. 153).

I recently had a woman in Taco Bell comment on my arm tattoo, which celebrates God's providence in my life with flowers and the Chinese characters for *God gives* using the name of the ancient Chinese God, Shangdi. (Matthew 6:28-30 reminds me not to worry because God provides: *See how the flowers of the field grow. They do not labor or spin. Yet I tell you that not even Solomon in all his splendor was dressed like one of these. If that is how God clothes the grass of the field, which is here today and tomorrow is thrown into the fire, will he not much more clothe you—you of little faith?)*

"That's a lovely tattoo," she told me. "My opinion is that people who really care about their health don't do things like get tattoos and piercings. But it's pretty." I smiled and thanked her. I know she judged an act that she views as dangerous, while in my mind the act itself upheld the ideal that I know to be true: I care about and celebrate my health daily. I decided not to tell her that people who really care about their health don't eat at Taco Bell, because perhaps she was eating there for the same reason I was—a greasy, hearty taco was the only thing that was going to prevent me from throwing up a recent dose of medication that set my stomach aflame. At least, that was the grace-laden assumption I had made when explaining my own, highly justifiable behavior.

Rolling forward...

seventeen | I can see clearly now, the rain is out

Our strength is often composed of the weaknesses we're damned if we're going to show.

Mignon Mclaughlin

I don't know what it is about teaching that makes me want to take better care of myself. Perhaps my personal disdain for hypocrisy is to blame; how can I, as a role model, encourage my students to grow into responsible, well-informed, and hardworking individuals if I am ignoring my own health?

Or perhaps they have pushed me to take risks. When I showed up on the first day of school in August 2005, I had never taught junior high and had hippopotamus-sized butterflies in my stomach. And that turned out to be one of the best decisions I ever made.

So I decide this December to go to the National Institutes of Health and enroll myself in the cysteamine eye drop study.

I am a little late to this ball game. The drops were first offered to me in 1990, while they were experimental and very much unproven as a viable treatment for cystine crystal buildup in the eyes. As a child, not only did I detest the idea of putting drops in my eyes at any time (let alone every waking hour as prescribed), but I also didn't believe my eyes to be too negatively impacted by my disease. Throughout my childhood, the sunlight didn't seem to bother me tremendously, at least not compared to others I came in contact with at cystinosis conferences. Most of the time, I am still stubborn enough that I don't even wear sunglasses outside.

But I have heard of people going blind due to the cystine. This brings up a third theory as to why I might be so eager to get the drops now: it took no more than a week in the classroom for me to realize that I have found my calling. I want to continue to see the beautiful faces of my students each and every day.

I pretend that it's no big deal. I tell my roommate, coworkers, and family that I am heading to Washington, D.C. to get an experimental medication. Because it's no big deal, I don't need anyone to come with me. I have no idea that I might need a shoulder to cry on.

It's already pretty embarrassing to be staying at The Children's Inn while in Bethesda, but I figure, at least (since I am traveling alone) I won't see anyone I know. (Actually, I can not emphasize enough that The Children's Inn is a huge blessing. Years later when I return to the NIH at the age of thirty, I am distraught to learn that the cut-off age for the Inn is twenty-six.)

When I arrive on that atypically snowy day in late December, I hop on the subway and successfully make my way to my destination. (Navigating the subway system is a lot easier, than, say, finding my way around a Paris airport—as I will discover during another solo travel experience in which I could also really use a shoulder to cry on or a hand to hold.)

Once inside The Children's Inn, I unpack some of my toiletries and lay down to mentally prepare for the following day's appointment. Staring at the ceiling, I marvel at how I have brought myself here in order to get on the hourly eye drops that years ago I had refused to even consider. At that time, putting cold liquid in my eyes every waking hour had seemed unthinkable. Now, it seems like a privilege.

Not one to lie down for long, I grab my light, California coat and make my way back to the subway. It is time to explore.

I breathe in the cold air and enjoy the centuries-old architecture of the buildings around me. I'm proud to be from the West Coast, but everything feels so new and modern there. As a history teacher, it's slightly disappointing to realize that nothing in my hometown will be hugely historical until long after I'm gone.

Three hours later, I am back at the Inn, my body and ego mildly bruised from a slip on the ice. I check in with the front desk and let the employee there know that I will be heading up the street to the NIH for

152

my appointment fairly early in the morning. Since the Inn is so intimately connected to the hospital, it requests this kind of information.

"Would you like an escort?" the woman behind the desk asks me.

With prideful eyes, I scoff at her question. "No, I think I can manage. Thank you."

The next morning, I head to my appointment in the snow. Thoroughly enjoying my walk, I muse at the receptionist's question the night before. *Maybe a child would need help,* I think to myself. *But me? I am an adult. A college graduate. A full-time teacher. A cross-country independent traveler.* (Are you seeing a pattern? How many times will I have to remind myself that *pride goeth before a fall* before it actually sinks into my stubborn skin?)

My appointment is routine. As is typical, I am made to feel like someone's science experiment—but unlike your typical lab rat, I am happy to be a part of it all. When I am nearly done with the appointment, I am handed my first bottle of eye drops and I feel a great sense of triumph. Until the ophthalmologist comes in one last time.

"I want to dilate your eyes and do a few more pictures," she tells me. I groan. I hate having my eyes dilated. I put up with it (only barely) because I can see the figurative light at the end of the tunnel, and I know I will soon be left to my own devices and on my way home. Home, where I'm not constantly reminded of what ails.

Once the pictures are taken, I am shuffled back out to the waiting area and front desk of the ophthalmology department. I look at the nurse through blurred eyes. She is telling me that I will need to return in a year's time for a follow-up appointment, but I am already thinking about what I will have for dinner and trying not to dwell on my upcoming task of putting drops in my eyes every waking hour because I am not normal. Her last question makes my humiliation complete.

"Do you need me to call someone from The Children's Inn to come get you?" she asks, already reaching for the phone.

"No," I say, this time firmly and without niceties. Why does everyone think I am incapable of walking three blocks? "I'm fine and I can go on my own." I grab my purse, thank her for her help, and head out the door.

I am sure that the world in front of me must be some wolf-in-sheep's-clothing version of hell, for everything seems too bright for human eyes. The sun is shining, but the landscape is drenched in snow. The sun, in fact, is peaking through a break in the white clouds. I gasp and fall back on a bench outside the sliding glass exit doors. Everything is white. Everything is shiny. I am quite literally blinded by the light.

So I sit on that bench and I cry. I know that I am reacting to the dilation of my eyes, and that anyone would be uncomfortable in this situation. But I still feel certain that I have failed.

Two years after my trip to the NIH, I am no longer taking the eye drops. I guess I let life get in the way. Now I am planning my dream wedding: outside, in the summer, in a beautiful garden overflowing with flowers. I select the Gardens at Heather Farm in Walnut Creek.

Wayne and I don't really discuss cystinosis. He knows that it exists, just as it seems like he always has. I know it doesn't matter. That is enough. He sees me take medication only rarely, and I am never, ever without my eye makeup while in his presence. In a lot of ways, I am a normal girl in love.

It isn't until the day before the wedding that I start to worry about my eyes. Will all my wedding photographs show me squinting in the sun? What terrible mistake have I made by deciding to have my wedding outside in the middle of the day and in the middle of the summer? Will I even be able to look up at my husband's face during the exchanging of vows?

The day of the wedding, though, I step outside in my wedding dress and know that my worries are insignificant. I don't need an overcast day to see clearly. I don't need dark sunglasses to see clearly. Excuse my stubbornness, but I don't even need a proven eye drop treatment to see clearly.

All I need is a clearly marked path to the man with whom I plan on spending the rest of my life. My eyes and my smile are both wide open that day.

Wayne has been overseas for about three months, having left me alone in our apartment in San Diego for the duration of his deployment. I pick up the phone and call the hospital on base.

"I'd like to make an ophthalmology appointment, please. I'm hoping to get some experimental drops through your pharmacy."

ruminations from the rink

Like my students inspiring me to take care of myself, albeit temporarily, my marriage led me to realize how much I wanted to see the world with my eyes wide open. When Wayne and I moved to the San Diego area following our wedding, we had a little over three months together before he was deployed with his Marine Expeditionary Unit to the Middle East. In his absence, I fought for months with the Naval Hospital in San Diego to get the cysteamine eye drops through its pharmacy and without going to the NIH. It was a long battle, but definitely worth it. I have been compliant with the eye drops ever since (and am now once again receiving them through the NIH).

But what both my first solo trip to the NIH and my wedding day indicated was a general need to appear strong. Despite the willingness (and eagerness) of The Children's Inn to help me through my experience, I was sure that I could do it alone. Likewise, despite Wayne's knowledge of cystinosis, I was determined not to let my perceived weaknesses show. He didn't know that I had ever been on hourly eye drops because while we were dating, I stopped them. Although he may have inspired me to resume, it wasn't until he was thousands of miles away that I actually renewed the fight to get this still-unapproved treatment back into my refrigerator.

Appearances are not what make a person strong. **We are strongest when we own up to our weaknesses and depend on those around us (and ultimately, God) as needed.** My pride in the face of my trip to the NIH (which went poorly) and my wedding (which was a success) point to a larger fault I have in generally denying myself help from those who love me, including my God.

I do not feel that I have fully embraced this lesson. But thankfully, I have let go of some of the areas in which I previously had a need to appear strong. I wear sunglasses when I need to and I put eye drops in my eyes in front of my husband. (He is still not permitted to see me throw up after taking cysteamine, however.)

Rolling forward…

eighteen | lessons learned from a healthy cat's seizure

Life is not meant to be easy, my child; but take courage: it can be delightful.

George Bernard Shaw

My husband and I are crazy cat ladies. (He just corrected me. He is a crazy cat *guy.*)

Well, at the very least, we are certainly headed in that direction. For the first three years of our marriage, we adopt a cat a year. Although we've refrained since, I'm sure it's only a matter of time.

In 2009, when we are shopping around for the perfect third cat, I am at first adamant that three really is too many. But it's our third cat that proves to be a story of irony, survival, and proving-everyone-wrong.

We are looking for a cat that will be what our other two are not: a cuddly lap companion. After going to a couple shelters, we end up at a facility in San Diego. Wayne and I are both awed at the place; there are large, themed rooms for the animals, filled with cat furniture and toys galore. I imagine that even *I* could live here contently.

Almost immediately, I zero in on a beautiful feline with only three legs. As I gaze at him through the glass, my heart melts. One of the shelter employees is in the room giving the cats some attention, and this orange-and-white treasure clearly craves every second of her time. The employee cradles him in her arms and he nuzzles his face into her armpit. I am in love. Unable to walk well on his own, this cat requires the extra care that I want so desperately to give.

Unfortunately, this cat is "bonded" to his sister and cannot be adopted alone. Since we are at least certain that we don't want four cats, we have to pass. I keep my eyes open for another special needs kitty, but the process is overwhelming in a shelter so large. An adoption specialist comes to help us and take us through the different rooms, and I tell her of my desire to care for a cat with medical challenges, pointing out that the only reason we are passing up the three-legged sweetheart is because we don't want to adopt two. She takes us into a room with a variety of cats and points out one that has kidney problems.

"Oh, I'd be fine with that!" My response is quick and enthusiastic. "I have kidney problems, too! I had a transplant a decade ago."

The woman's demeanor, previously one of keen assistance, quickly changes. I can sense her pity almost immediately, as I have had more than two decades of experience sensing such emotion from people who learn of my situation.

"Ah. Well, good for you! It's so great that you are here and willing to give. But special needs people shouldn't adopt special needs pets. It's simply too much work. You need to take care of yourself and adopt a healthy, hearty cat that can be your comfort."

Surprisingly, my jaw doesn't drop to the floor. My right hand doesn't raise to slap her silly. I am not left speechless. In my mind, I know her words reflect an ignorance of how much "special needs people" truly have to offer. In my heart, though, her words, "special needs people shouldn't adopt special needs pets" sting terribly.

"Your medical bills are probably overwhelming," she adds. "Better to not get a cat with a situation that will strain your pocketbook as well. Take care of yourself, honey."

I pick my battles. This is not one I am willing to have, especially given that my potential contender feels pity for her opponent. It is our money and we can choose to adopt any cat in the place; however, I let her words fall heavy on my shoulders and turn away from the special needs rooms. We go into one of the larger rooms, surround ourselves with healthy cats, and choose the one that can't get enough of our attention. She is beautiful in her own right, though whole; her four legs and healthy kidneys remind me that I will not have to give her as much care as I have in me to give. We fill out the paperwork and pay for our purchase and eagerly head home to introduce our other two cats to the newest addition, a Russian Blue mix we name Mrs. Edgar Allan Poe.

It is about two months later that Poe has her first seizure.

Wayne and I are sitting on the couch, watching some mindless television after long days at work. Poe is in her usual spot, cuddled between us for warmth and sleeping soundly. When she starts twitching suddenly, it catches both of us by surprise. She jolts up and races off the couch, running furiously in all directions and hitting plenty of furniture along the way. Wayne catches her and holds her violently twitching body in his arms; she starts foaming at the mouth and her eyes roll back in her head. I fight back tears as I watch the baby of our family die; I am certain we will be back to two cats within minutes.

To our surprise, the twitching eventually stops and her eyes return to their proper position, although they appear both glazed over and terrified at the same time. Her body feels limp; the moment Wayne sits her on the floor she falls over in a way reminiscent of a man disembarking a bar stool after he has had one too many... and then five more.

We take Poe to the pet emergency room and await the results of many tests. She is put on IV fluids and fails many of the clinic's neurological tests, although she improves with every passing hour.

The final diagnosis: epilepsy.

The vet confirms that although she has had an epileptic seizure and it will take her some time to regain stability, she is fine. The fit, he claims, was something she won't remember. There isn't any recommended treatment because there is no medication that will stop the epileptic attacks, but only something that can reduce their number; since we have only witnessed one in the past couple months, it seems unlikely that they are a frequent occurrence. We take our baby home and find ourselves doting over her and keeping an anxious eye in her direction; she still maintains her position as our neediest household item, demanding warmth and attention more than our other two cats, the litter box, whatever is about to boil over on the stove, and the glass-top and fingerprint-prone dining room table needing Windex combined.

ruminations from the rink

My thoughts occasionally go back to the woman at the animal shelter who so callously told me that special needs people shouldn't have special needs pets. In her effort to sell me a cat with a clean bill of health, she inadvertently sent me home with a case of feline epilepsy. The shelter employee, of course, does not deserve my haughty thoughts. No one does. But what she represents is a stigma often attached to people with special needs: we are takers, not givers.

Too often, I think, this even becomes an excuse for those of us who should know better. The "poor me" mentality gets the best of us, and we become the takers that we so resent being labeled. The reality is that God created each of us to be there for one another, to do unto others, and to love and give selflessly. The time and affection (and unconditional love) that I so easily lavish on Poe too frequently does not extend into the realm of my own species. I am short with people, I search for specks of dust in their character while my own is littered with planks (Matthew 7:3-5), and I am greedy with their time and love but not generous with my own.

It doesn't matter what our condition. We are all obliged to give something of ourselves to those around us. I have learned two important lessons from Poe the cat. Firstly, the needs of others aren't always immediately apparent. **And sometimes those believed to be caretakers are actually those most eager to give.** Let's put aside our wonderful, but inhuman pets for a moment. Who can you lavish with love today? Whatever your own unique circumstances, you have something to offer, and there is someone out there who needs exactly what you have to give.

Rolling forward…

nineteen | beginnings in ends

There will come a time when you believe everything is finished.
That will be the beginning.

Louis L'Amour

I'm writing in my online journal. I know that many people in my life know the story (as the newspapers are telling it) and are waiting to hear my thoughts.

But it's been a while since I've been able to find the words. The intensity of their inadequacy has left my fingers still, my keyboard dusty. When something so tragic and unreal touches your life—or, more accurately, crashes down on it like a sledge hammer—what constitutes an appropriate written response?

Maybe there isn't one. But being the aspiring writer that I am, I suppose it is inevitable that I will eventually try.

> *I started this blog with every intention of devoting the next year of my life to physical endurance and reporting my success here. But, as the Proverb goes, "Many are the plans in a man's heart, but it is the Lord's purpose that prevails." My plans were put on hold.*

> *On the afternoon of August 31, I was finishing up a day of teaching my sixth, seventh, and eighth graders and preparing to start Study Hall for K-8 students. The secretary found me and told me my husband was on the phone.*

He asked me if I was sitting down. Ever the optimist, I briefly thought I was about to be on the receiving end of some very good news. Even so, I asked, "What's wrong?"

Thirty seconds later, the secretary and the principal were hurriedly shuffling me into the principal's office and transferring the call. I don't think I've ever gone into clinical shock, and I don't think I did then. But I know I must have been a sight to see, because my entire body was shaking uncontrollably.

"Mom and dad have been murdered," he told me.

I thought he had misspoken. My mother-in-law had recently been diagnosed with advanced breast cancer that had spread to her bones, and though I certainly never wanted to hear the news that her condition had gone south, I assumed he had meant to say that his mom was in the hospital in critical condition or worse.

As the phone call continued, though, and more details were given, it became evident that I had heard correctly. I pushed the question I had on my mind to the back of my head. You never want to believe that someone you know could be capable of such hatred and violence.

But whether I thought it or said it, that question was eventually answered.

"The police are looking for Drew." (Drew, Wayne's brother, was actually already in custody. But we didn't know that at the time.)

All this brings me back to the inability to put words to it all. I mean, what can you say? I loved my mother- and father-in-law. I have all the usual regrets; we didn't see them enough (although we had been tentatively planning a Labor Day weekend trip—a trip that, ironically, we ended up making), I didn't usually talk when Wayne and Marilyn had their weekly phone call, and the last time I saw Scott I hadn't told him how much I appreciated his quiet strength. I disagreed with them on some things, but I never explicitly told Marilyn how much I appreciated her care and concern for her family. When several hundred people came to their memorial, I took comfort in knowing that I was not alone. We all craved the opportunity to be given one last chance to say goodbye.

As someone who typically feels things very deeply, I've struggled with the near surreality of it all. Even so, I keep reliving moments I didn't actually experience. The attack came as a surprise to Scott; Marilyn, however, was not caught unaware. By all likely accounts (including Drew's confession), she witnessed her husband's plight before trying to escape what would become her own. Over and over in my head, I imagine that scene and her terror; I try to will it away and pray it gone but it stays. While at the farm looking through pictures for the memorial slide show, I found one of a young Drew with a scythe in the fields; a feeling of nausea swept over me since this was the murder weapon used on his father. The scene has finally inundated my dreams—much later than I expected, but there nonetheless.

I returned to a full week of work last Monday and found apparent comfort in overworking. I get home from teaching around 5:00 and then spend the next six hours working my second job, a telecommuting associate editor position. By Wednesday I realized that I was killing myself, but I didn't know what else to do. At least it kept my mind away from everything else, even if it left me mentally and physically exhausted each day. I found it easier to complain about the poor writing that I have to fix than to cry about a situation that I cannot.

This morning, though, on the first free day I've had since the incident, I opened my eyes and I breathed. I exhaled anger. I inhaled pain.

In the six months that have passed since Wayne's brother committed an unthinkable crime, a lot has happened to remind us that life goes on. We have just ushered in a new year (2011). Wayne has connected with his birth mother, first in Utah for Christmas and then at our apartment for her weekend visit; I've re-found my rhythm at school and have been offered an Upper School Dean position for next year; and we've signed a new lease on our apartment, confirming that we plan on staying put in the Bay Area for now.

But life going on doesn't mean that the past is left behind. I believe that the past follows us into the present, and that our whole lives are a conglomeration of the old and the new. We've had visits from investigators, we still have the farm to deal with, and I recently made banana bread using Marilyn's mixing bowls.

If it seems like I haven't moved on, I haven't. The nightmares have become infrequent, but the daytime thoughts have not. Nearly every day I think of the murders as I drive home from school; as recently as today I told myself, "Don't think about Marilyn's last moments," but I did.

ruminations from the rink

Honestly, I was never sure how my mother-in-law felt about me while she was alive, although I never doubted her heart for others. It was only after her death that I learned from some of her friends that she spoke highly of me. It was so humbling to learn that Marilyn, one of the toughest people I ever met—and someone who cured herself of cancer at least once, and perhaps twice (the autopsy did not show the disease)—felt me to be strong.

She and I had very different philosophies about health and healing. But she inspires me to rely on the healing principles we had in common: faith and hope. She never treated me as a victim or as sick (because truly, I am not), and she never took on the victim mentality herself, even after being diagnosed with stage IV cancer. Her faith told her that she was always exactly in the place where God wanted her to be.

Scott and Marilyn will forever remain in my heart. I will carry my parents-in-law with me until I see them in heaven. **Their deaths remind me to have a passion for life that simply cannot be stifled.** When I think about Marilyn's last moments now, more than a year and a half later, I try to remember to gratefully live from this moment forward. In a video interview from the farm shot shortly before her death, Marilyn reminded us all what a gift it is to breathe in God's air and enjoy God's creation. It's that simple. I'm doing what I love and experiencing abundant blessings that I don't deserve. That is all we can do every day—because whether you have cancer, cystinosis, or are completely healthy, you can never know how much longer you have.

Life is filled with curve balls. "Many are the plans in a person's heart, but it is the Lord's purpose that prevails" (Proverbs 19:21).

Rolling forward…

twenty | celebrating the birthday I would never live to see (part 2)

Old age is the most unexpected of all the things that can happen to a man.

Leon Trotsky

Natalis grate numeras?

(Do you count your birthdays thankfully?)

Horace

Until my twenty-ninth birthday, I never think of myself as a survivor. You see, it isn't until my twenty-ninth birthday that I realize that, barring some tragic and unexpected event, I will live to see age thirty.

Until relatively recently, cystinosis was considered a children's disease. But I am thankful that this has changed and is still changing.

The disease has been a source of both victory and defeat. A particularly poignant example of both comes while I am teaching in a sixth grade Social Studies classroom in a Southern California public school near the Marine Corps base my husband is stationed at. It is "Say No To Drugs" week, and as I stand in front of my thirty-four kids, preparing to start the day's lesson, a student comes in with a stack of red ribbons, being distributed to all the teachers. With only a brief interruption, she instructs me that I am to pin the ribbon on my clothing to demonstrate my solidarity with this important cause.

As a junior high teacher, you quickly learn that it's best to not miss a beat, for a moment of letting your guard down can lead to a class period of preteen chaos. I continue my lesson while at the same time saying a fervent, selfish, silent prayer: *God, please make my fingers work. Just this once. While all my kids are watching. Make unfastening this safety pin easy for me.*

But it isn't. I stand there, struggling with the pin, all the while continuing to talk about the ancient Mesopotamians. My mind is being worked to its capacity, multitasking words and thoughts. "The ancient Sumerians were able to accomplish great things in the areas of building and farming once they developed the wheel." *Please, let them believe this is taking so long because I'm talking, rather than thinking about what I am doing.* "Their writing system was also innovative, and this allowed them to keep detailed records." *Oh, there's no way I'll get this safety pin open. I couldn't even button my own pants this morning! I should just give up.* "With their writing system, they produced the Epic of Gilgamesh, one of the oldest written works in the world." *This is ridiculous. I hope none of my students ever gives me an apple, and discovers I can't swallow, either!*

I sometimes marvel at the fact that I am still on this planet. Going strong? Perhaps that is the wrong choice of words. Now muscle wasting has taken over as my primary concern, and I can no longer grip a pencil for any prolonged period of time, button my own jeans consistently, swallow certain foods with ease, or—of course—flawlessly unfasten and fasten a safety pin. But recently it's occurred to me that I'm a fighter, something I never thought I'd say. And stranger still, I'm powerfully optimistic, in spite of never thinking of myself as such. I take pride in the victories and hold out hope in the face of defeat. I am less afraid to ask for help and share with others how cystinosis has positively impacted my life. Surrounded by supportive, loving family and friends and a thriving cystinosis community through online social networking is a luxury that I know helps me get through each day.

Which brings me back to that darn safety pin. After several anxious moments, I get that thing on with all eyes watching. My day goes a little easier, and I hold my head a little higher at the thought of my small, but significant, victory. That red ribbon comes to symbolize not only teenagers resisting drug-related peer pressure, but my own ability to successfully perform mundane tasks with no help whatsoever.

It is in light of this dangerous line of thinking that I return home. My husband asks if I need him to take the red ribbon off. "No," I say proudly, "I unfastened and fastened it myself earlier to get it on." And so I sit, on the couch and completely focused, with no one watching. After a good five minutes of attempting a task that had earlier been a source of such confidence, I tearfully look at Wayne. "I need you," I say.

"I'm glad," he says, and with a smile he easily takes the ribbon off my shirt.

Yes, I do think I'll make it to thirty.

ruminations from the rink

I believe a person with cystinosis experiences a great physical and emotional victory the day after a successful kidney transplant. In some ways, it feels like everything is behind us, for from diagnosis we are told this is the organ we have to worry about the most. By September 1999, a month after my own transplant, I made a surprising realization: those college applications I had filled out the previous year, the period of anxious waiting, that acceptance letter that I had been most proud of—it all actually *meant* something. Previously, the letter had been mere words on a page, words to offer me some self-satisfaction and yet words that were part of some far-off, idealistic dream that would somehow persist in the future but never be part of my reality. Then, as I prepared to attend the University of California at Berkeley, I had one thought and one thought only: I'm going to live through college.

And live, I did. I experienced so much of what I had missed out on in high school—a social scene, the energy to participate in a variety of events, and the stamina to come home from a full day of classes and study (though, particularly in that first year, I didn't always do so) and attend late-night pizza parties in the shared lounge. At one point, I casually told my roommate that I had to take a few days off to have a stent placed in my Superior Vena Cava, the main vein into the heart, and my reply to her wide-eyed reaction was merely, "Oh, it's no big deal. I'll be back. You're stuck with me for the long haul."

At the same time and perhaps ironically given how I viewed life as a child, I never thought too far into the future following my transplant, and I dealt off and on with bouts of depression over having surpassed expectations. When one of my friends with cystinosis died while I was at Berkeley, I found myself often looking at a photograph with the two of us posing, in a park, with two other women with cystinosis. The reality is that I am the only one in that photograph left standing, which has been the case since my friend's death more than eight years ago. It was at that time that I realized, *What now? I'm going to live, and contrary to what I believed for so much of my life, the challenges don't end with a working kidney. Things are going to get harder.*

When shortly after college, my eyes became so painful due to cystine crystal buildup that I started hourly eye drops—a process that, in order to stave away blindness, I must continue for the rest of my life—I still felt I could do it all alone. My thyroid was next to go, when a blood test showed an alarmingly harmful deficiency of the hormone the organ produces. I married my high school sweetheart in July 2007 and remember distinctly thinking on my wedding day that I should be able to get a couple years of wedded bliss in before my body failed me completely.

But I am still here.

And furthermore, despite periods of living alone and still being able to do most things on my own, I have never *been* alone. **When I ask for help in my weakest moments, I become stronger.**

A wise friend once told me to "cherish what was given." For those of us living with difficult medical conditions from birth, we can either cherish what we have or lament what we don't. I can dwell on the fact that I count the people I know who are living with cystinosis and are over the age of forty on one hand, or I can express my immense gratitude at having lived thirty wonderful years. (I mean, imagine this… my parents were told I'd only live ten. I just read a recent news article that said I'd probably succumb to death before the age of forty. But I haven't even had a mid-life crisis yet!) We don't come with expiration dates. We are given the blessing of life while we have it. Cherish what was given.

I cherish both those things that I can do on my own and those things that remind me that I never have to go it alone.

Rolling forward…

twenty-one | regret

I have the unpleasant experience of having a flexible scope put up my nose and down my throat. (No amount of literary sugar-coating can both soften the language and maintain the integrity of the event itself.) As no fewer than six doctors crowd into the room, I eat and drink all manner of disgusting food and liquid, wondering how my swallowing can be accurately evaluated with the additional hindrance of a tube partially blocking my airway.

What is discovered is that I have a weak tongue, along with compromised throat walls. The silver lining is that there is nothing wrong with my esophagus or larynx, and my vocal cords perform as they are supposed to. (This good news does nothing to diminish the creepiness of actually seeing my vocal cords vibrate, on the big screen, as I am instructed to speak awkward noises worthy of some Amazonian tree frog.)

It does not surprise me that along with other muscle wasting, I have experienced degeneration in this area; however, I am optimistic about partial reversal. After all, when I discovered six months ago that I had lost my ability to gargle or suck from a straw, I worked at it every day—and now I have little difficulty. But I know that cystinosis is progressive, and that I have done untold damage by not taking cysteamine for much of my twenties.

I am back where it all began (not for me, but for modern-day cystinosis research): the National Institutes of Health in Bethesda, near our nation's capital. I imagine Dr. Schneider working here in the 1960s and learning that the secret to cystinosis rests with the cystine crystals that build up in the cells. I remember my most recent trip, when I broke down and cried in the reflective brightness of a pale sky meeting wet, white snow. This time, I am armed with less intracellular cystine than was ever imagined possible for someone with cystinosis in the 1960s, confidence, prepared questions, and my husband's hand in mine. I walk in the hospital like I own it. I have cystinosis, but I am *in it to win it,* determined to beat it at its own game, confident that there are answers if only someone cares enough about a rare disease community only a few thousand strong (at most) to find them.

The first day of my three-day appointment seems to go fairly well. I face my fears and take a ride in the CT scanner, I give an unreal amount of blood, and I put my chin in the slit lamp contraption at the ophthalmologist's office. She tells me that my eyes are moderately impacted by crystals and that I will do better to use the NIH-formulated cysteamine eye drops rather than the ones I've been getting from a compounding pharmacy. This is fine by me; being part of the ongoing eye study at the NIH will save me close to $200 a month on medication. She reminds me to put the drops in as close to every waking hour that I can. I don't bother to say that eye drops and eye liner don't mix, but I certainly think it to myself. Nonetheless, she assures me that imminent blindness is not my fate and that what I have been doing has kept the crystals somewhat at bay. A trip to the dentist reveals that I do not have the dental problems that can occur in people with cystinosis.

It's a good thing the first day is so positively uneventful, because the second day hits me like a strong punch in the stomach. It makes sense: if pride goeth before a fall, it is high time for me to be reminded that I haven't lived a life of perfect compliance and there are very real consequences for going ten years without oral cysteamine.

I have some trouble with the lung test. The machine used to measure my lung capacity and function is difficult for me to tolerate. I have lost enough muscle strength in my lips that I cannot form a tight seal around the tube. I am embarrassed. The test reveals that my capacity isn't too bad (around ninety percent) but my function is closer to seventy percent. In addition to that difficult news, I learn that yesterday's CT scan has revealed some sort of mass on the exterior of my left lung.

But the real challenge comes with a barium swallowing test.

The most immediately apparent manifestation of my progressive disease is in the changes that have taken place in my speech and swallowing. My voice has significant power behind it for someone my age with cystinosis (I do yell my way through daily classes and weekly playground lunch duties with junior high students, after all), but due to lip and tongue muscle weakness, enunciation has become more challenging. Over time, I have gradually reduced the number of tough, chewy foods I consume owing to the fact that swallowing has become more difficult. I seem to cough more frequently after taking in liquids as well, a troubling fact that I have done my best to ignore.

As I have said many times in my life, however, ignorance is not bliss. Having endured a scope up my nose and down my esophagus just last year, I wonder how bad this test can really be. I am told that I will be swallowing substances of varying thickness and containing a radioactive material. As I stand in front of an x-ray machine and take in the substances, the path they take down into my stomach will be viewable on the screen in front of me.

In my case, though, not everything makes it into my stomach as it is supposed to.

When I swallow the first syringe-full of relatively loose liquid, it is clearly evident to everyone in the room staring expectantly at the screen that much of the liquid is remaining pooled in the back of my throat. More troubling still, a certain amount of it has gone down what many of us like to refer to as the "wrong pipe"—my trachea.

I stiffen and put my game face on. I give Wayne a look that says simply, *Watch out. The stubborn side is about to rear its lovely head.*

The doctor requests that I try for a stronger swallow. The pool gets smaller, but residual amounts of liquid remain.

"We'll give you a substance with a yogurt-like consistency now," she says, "but in light of what we're seeing, we will skip the graham cracker altogether."

I am upset. What is she implying? I eat crackers outside of the hospital without major issue. Why not here? I remain stoic.

The syringe is refilled and I swallow something that tastes and feels a bit like vanilla pudding. This time, when I swallow, more of the substance properly goes down my esophagus. Some is left at the back of my throat, and a small amount takes the wrong path.

The doctor's evaluation is nothing short of dreadful. She tells me that I should avoid solid foods and loose liquids in order to minimize my risk of aspirating what I consume and then developing bacterial pneumonia as a result. You may wonder what there is left to eat if I'm avoiding both solids and liquids.

"You should stick to textures that are like pudding," she tells me. "You can puree solid foods and add a thickener to loose liquids."

I try to tell her that food is delicious. She tries to tell me that life is precious. Must these two undeniable facts be in opposition?

We have a conversation about quality of life versus quantity of life. I point out that I have had bacterial pneumonia before and that it is treatable with antibiotics. Nevertheless, she is insistent that I avoid aspiration as much as possible. I know that's why she isn't letting me eat the graham crackers; she is concerned about my safety. I utilize my limited knowledge of the *if you don't use it, you lose it* principle and say that surely I need to continue chewing and swallowing solids in order to build that musculature up. She points out that unlike skeletal muscles, esophageal muscles are smooth and not necessarily rehabilitative. My reasoning is flawed.

I tell her I won't give up something that brings such joy. Not yet. In her report she labels me as resistant.

That night, Wayne and I go out to dinner and I order a steak and savor every bite, chew, and swallow.

Some years ago I made a ridiculous attempt to read every fiction book on *The New York Times'* bestseller list. It was a short-lived attempt. I found myself captured by engaging plots, enamored by writing styles, and awed by far-reaching (yet short-lived) life applications. Some, like *Tuesdays with Morrie,* were stories of life fading. Others, like *The Life of Pi,* were fantastical tales of life survival. I found little enlightenment in *Everything is Illuminated* and unexplainable sadness in the quest for truth of the author of *Eat, Pray, Love.*

None had the impact of a book I read in seventh grade, *Flowers for Algernon*. This is the story of a man (Charlie) with severe cognitive delays that scientists cure, through experiments on a lab rat named Algernon. As a gift, Charlie (with his new talents to seemingly learn everything from rocket science to philosophy to how to communicate using intimidating vocabulary) is given the rat to keep as a pet, and he chronicles his second-chance life full of new opportunities and new abilities. But after a time, the protagonist sees with horror that his new life will not be sustainable: Algernon, the beloved lab rat representing all that can be overcome, starts to deteriorate. The rat seems confused and can no longer navigate the complicated maze of buttons and countless steps to get to his water and food. Each day, a new step is forgotten, and more assistance is needed. And our hero can only await what will surely be his fate as well: the loss of the mind that he has only begun to enjoy. Charlie chronicles his life as it slowly goes the way of Algernon the lab rat, soon unable to write coherent sentences in his journal. The reader feels his pain as life slips through his fingers. The story, though fiction, is made all the more engaging by its first-person style, complete with simple vocabulary, misspellings, and grammatically incorrect sentence fragments (before the cure), complex sentences with difficult vocabulary and perfect spelling (at the height of health), and a slow regression back to the former style. I remember thinking as a twelve-year-old, "Wow, this author can *write.*"

My husband can write. His stories come alive with creativity and imagination. I bought him a book containing a collection of writing prompts to stretch and challenge one's ability in every possible way. His first attempt was fantastic. Mine fell flat. Decent grammar, impeccable spelling, elaborate sentences, descriptive adjectives, an adequate dilemma, climax, and resolution—but no heart, no energy, no... oomph. Fiction writing may be my dream but it is also my nemesis: I am Noah Webster to my husband's J.R.R. Tolkien—and yet, not even a Webster-grade wordsmith.

This year has thus far been a year of wordy reflection. These are words that have been caught somewhere in between the place where they originate and the tears of gratitude that sometimes fall when I think about the past thirty years God has given me to live. There are parts of my physical body that are deteriorating, much like what happened to the real Morrie or fictional Charlie. But thanks to the healing hems of the garment of Jesus, I am perpetually holding on to a life redeemed.

Maybe I can't pen the great American novel, but I can chronicle life. Even if the muscles in my fingers become too weak to use a writing implement for any sustained period of time without great difficulty, the keyboard remains my ink, and this, my journal.

I could look back at my choices with sadness. But I choose today to regret nothing. I know that life has been, is, and will be nothing short of miraculous. It is a miracle that I am alive, and I thank God for how I was created.

ruminations from the rink

The paradox of regret is that it so easily consumes us, and yet it serves no greater purpose. **When we regret, we waste precious moments of our present dwelling on a past that we cannot change.** I know I struggle at times with regret, especially with regards to medication noncompliance earlier in my life. When I allow myself these unhealthy thoughts, it goes something like this:

If only I had taken my medicine in my early twenties, I would still be able to pinch my fingers together, snap, grip items both small and large, deal with clasps on necklaces, and button and unbutton even stiff clothing fasteners with ease.

If only I had taken my medicine in my early twenties, it wouldn't be possible to feel bone when pinching the now completely atrophied area between my thumb and index finger.

If only I had taken my medicine in my early twenties, I wouldn't have to worry about people understanding certain sounds when I verbally communicate.

If only I had taken my medicine in my early twenties, my lips would be strong enough to tighten around a breathing machine tube or a drinking straw.

If only I had taken my medicine in my early twenties, my lungs would be operating at a normal capacity.

Do you see what I'm doing when I go through this mental exercise? I'm focusing on what could have been.

But it's not what is. I made a serious mistake; I see that now. Whether or not I could have preserved all these functions, I cannot know. Some of my friends who have been very consistent about taking cysteamine throughout their lives and from a young age have similar problems. Nonetheless, I know I erred. Go figure. I am human.

(And sometimes, just sometimes, I look at it like this: If only I had taken my medicine in my early twenties, I might have shied away from close relationships owing to my fear of others picking up the odor of Cystagon. For in my early twenties, I was very insecure. Had I been taking my medicine, perhaps I never would have allowed the rekindling of a relationship that ultimately resulted in marriage.)

I do believe that everything has turned out exactly the way God intended it to. My free will resulted in a problematic choice. *Man is condemned to be free.* But what is most important is not the mistake, but what I learn from it. While regret pushes us backward, lessons propel us forward.

I want to take nothing that I have now for granted. I go up and down three flights of stairs several times a day. My legs are strong. I give lectures on a subject that I love. My voice is understandable. I am able to grip many things with my knuckles, and with this new technique it is rare that I need to ask for assistance with buttons. My body has adapted. I cherish meals with family and friends. I'm still eating.

All of these things could someday change. But if I am compliant with my cysteamine moving forward—and despite my stubborn streak that occasionally serves me well—I will maximize the likelihood that when I am forty, I won't look back at my thirties the way I now sometimes look back at my twenties: with regret. I am still learning what it means to be kind to myself and recognizing that it serves no purpose for me to treat my twenties with condemnation. There are many everyday functions that cystinosis can claim: sight, voice, swallowing, walking, strength. Now I have a better understanding of my role in fighting to preserve them. My twenties have ensured that I will live smarter in my thirties. In the words of Søren Kierkegaard, "Life must be understood backwards; but... it must be lived forwards."

My hope for all of you is that you are able to accept mistakes for what they are: valuable learning experiences and opportunities for a wiser future.

Rolling forward...

epilogue | beautiful flaws

Every good and perfect gift is from above,
coming down from the Father of the heavenly lights,
who does not change like shifting shadows.

James 1:17

For you created my inmost being;
you knit me together in my mother's womb.

Psalm 139:13

Cystinosis causes a buildup of the amino acid cystine in all the cells of the body. This amino acid, so benign in individuals without cystinosis, crystallizes into toxic levels and destroys cells and organs in someone like me.

My eyes are naturally saturated with cystine crystals, though this saturation can be unnaturally reduced with the hourly cysteamine eye drops that are designed to dissolve them. These crystals cause eye discomfort and photophobia and can even ultimately lead to vision problems and blindness if the retina is impacted. I know of several people with cystinosis who have undergone cornea transplants and a couple who are blind.

This would seem to be a nuisance on top of everything else that someone with cystinosis must consider. And, well, it is. The eye drops—which at present in the United States must stay cold and spoil after a couple weeks—feel good. Even so, who wants to put eye drops in every waking hour? It is tiresome and inconvenient.

Sometimes it takes an outsider to remind us that even our flaws—nuisances, inconveniences, tiresome though they may be—are beautiful. I am seeing a new ophthalmologist today. He has never seen a patient with cystinosis.

I try to prepare him. "My eyes are saturated with crystals," I say.

"I've read about cystinosis," he responds, rather matter-of-factly. He is all business. "This will be interesting."

But no medical textbook, no patient warning, no prior experience can prepare him for what he will see when he looks at my eyes with a slit lamp. I hear him gasp.

"Oh! This...is...*wow*. It's beautiful!" He looks to my husband. "Have you seen this? You have to see this! It's amazing."

As I look at my new eye doctor, grinning from ear to ear in spite of himself, I have to blink back tears. They aren't tears of resentment, or tears of anger, or the tears that sometimes come from feeling misunderstood. They are tears of joy. Because he understands perfectly—my eyes are beautiful.

My eyes are a window into my illness. They sparkle with a substance that my whole body is full of—a substance that, despite its toxic nature, forms crystals as lovely as snowflakes. I am beautiful because of what I have endured, because of the blessings I have been handed, and because my uniqueness makes me *shine*.

As my ophthalmologist rushes out of the room to gather his colleagues for a look at his patient's eyes, I smile at my husband.

"Beautiful flaws," I say.

ruminations from the rink

When I was young, my mom made alphabet Bible verse quilts for Kirsten and me. The *E* verse was a shortened version of James 1:17: "Every good and perfect gift is from above." I often used those words to thank God for the good in life: my parents, my sister, teachers, kittens, and Disneyland trips. I liked the visual of good gifts showering down from heaven.

It wasn't until I was older that I thought to thank God for my disease.

Many of us are all too familiar with the bodily imperfections that we face on a daily basis. These flaws were not something that God intended for his perfect creation, but in His love He gave us a choice—and we chose our own path.

Humankind therefore brought much grief upon itself. But as Joseph says to his brothers in Genesis 50:20, "You meant it for evil; God meant it for good." Our inherently fallen nature has caused the damaged bodies that can bring us so much pain. But God orchestrates our lives before we are even a blip on an ultrasound. He has a perfect plan and purpose for us. And for those touched by chronic illness, that plan is good because it was authored by a God who is good.

Disease allows me to see miracles and rely more fervently on the God who made me. It has given me empathy for the sick and a powerful testimony to share. Being in and out of the hospital throughout my life has reminded me that God works through men and women who are devoted to caring for His people, just as Jesus cares for His people as the perfect Healer. When I gained a new life with the tragic loss of another and received my kidney transplant, I saw a snapshot of redemption: another person made the ultimate sacrifice for me. I praise God for entrusting me with these gifts.

My flaws are many, but they are beautiful. In the end, is this really a paradox? Or is it the story of a world in need of redemption and never-ending light and life?

Today I challenge you to find the good and perfect gifts that flow freely from heaven. Do you count your most challenging hardship (whatever that may be) as one of those gifts?

From my heart to yours, may you see today and always that from the trenches of hardship emerge joyous moments. Lace up those roller skates, friend, and live your life in light of the miraculous transformation that comes with experiencing miracles.